Rediscover

The Creator

Within

Rediscover The Creator Within

A Journey of Self-Discovery

Nicola Bowen

Creator Publishing

First Printing, 2022

The website address is: www.nicolabowen.com

Creator Publishing

ISBN-978-1-7399011-0-3

© Nicola Bowen 2022

Copies are available at a special rate for bulk orders. Contact the
sales development team via the website www.nicolabowen.com

For my girls

When life challenges you, I hope these words
will be a light and bring you comfort.
You have the strength to be buffeted by the storms of life,
to bend, bow and never break.
There is a universe of wisdom within you.
Be still.
Ask your questions and listen in the silence.
I love you.

Acknowledgements

To my beautiful friends:
Sharon, Alison, Katie, and Tink for your thoughts.
To Genna Clark, Create Results Coaching
for guiding me to the light.
To Karen for being my guinea pig–
even when it was painful.
To Alan for being my most prominent
teacher and support.

Masshoove hugs and heartfelt thanks to
Mo and Roger
for the many hours you have given
in deep contemplation and thought.
I love you all.

Introduction

How to step from a life run on auto-pilot
into your full power–
a life of bliss, love, and joy.

Enjoy the journey to discover your full potential.
Take control of your mind
to create the world around you
as you wish to see it.

Contents

one

Nicola's story

I appeared to have it all, a loving husband, two beautiful girls, and a stunning home. I greeted the world around me with a smile, but inside, I felt broken.

Middle-aged and consumed by sadness, I felt lost and without value or purpose. In my loneliest moments, I questioned, "what is the point?"

When life's onslaught appeared to reach its crescendo, fate faced my husband and me with no choice but to sell our dream family home. At the end of the heart-wrenching move day, I recall standing at the hotel's reception 'home' for the next few nights, feeling dazed and empty. We did not know where we would be living in the weeks and months ahead. My husband and daughters by my side, the girls with their beloved teddies, tucked tightly under their arms, and the receptionist asked, "What is your home address?"

I thought I would break. I didn't; I broke open.

Over the following days, all my fear and anger at life fell away. In its stead was peace, a wondrous feeling of love and awe for all things. I felt alive and free, ready to experience whatever life presented. I lived in this unfamiliar blissful state for many weeks, not understanding how I had arrived.

Over the ensuing months, life gradually returned to normal. Familiar unsettling feelings returned, but the fear and anxiety that had consumed me were gone.

This dramatic life change began my shift in awareness to the natural state of peace within us all. I understood who was responsible for the storms in my life and how to quiet them.

Rediscovering The Creator Within is my journey to return to the inviting space of presence, a step-by-step, back to basics understanding of what causes our suffering and how to move beyond it. It offers new ways to view life with simple techniques to move away from worry, stress, anxiety, and depression into a purposeful life lived to the fullest.

Nicola's story

Rediscover The Creator Within

two

Be still

A s I sit here writing to you, I reflect on how too often
life can appear fearful to so many. "Life is hard," is
often said, but is it meant to be? In my experience, we
honestly can live in bliss, love, and joy. Wherever you
start today, if this is your wish, this is possible for you too.
Through this book, I hope to guide you to see that there
are many ways to find peace of mind and live with a child-
like excitement about life.

After many years of suffering, I had an awakening,
having reached the point where I could no longer live
with all the painful thoughts I had allowed to dominate
my life. Without knowing how, my mind that had been so
busy for so long, was quiet. Space was created for
authentic thought of heart and mind, a space of bliss,
knowing all was and is, as it should be.

All my fear was gone, living in that stillness of mind for several months and present in each moment. I knew all could be added to my personal world, and nothing was ever taken away. Therein was the recognition that I alone create the world I see and feel around me. I understood that I could choose to direct my destiny at my will.

We are never truly broken, although it can sometimes feel that way. Look to the butterfly struggling to escape its cocoon following an awe-inspiring metamorphosis. Its fight for freedom brings strength and life to new wings as it launches on its inaugural flight. Perhaps in adversity, we, too, are prepared to step into our magnificence?

This book contains many pointers to still your mind and guides you towards presence, your state of innate peace and wellbeing. Try not to get hung up on and lost in words, as there will most likely be aspects of this book with which your mind takes time to come to grips. The meaning will become apparent to you at the right time. There are no rules to follow and no religion. Some words may jar or trigger a reaction within you as you read, yet you will come to an understanding beyond what, because, and why to the deeper reasons you feel emotion. Be kind and gentle with yourself. Be patient. Other words will raise questions. Be still. The answers will become apparent as you progress through this work.

It can be tempting to rush through each chapter, but every page has a message when your mind is still enough to see the meaning. You have taken the first step and picked up this book; perhaps now is your time for change and self-discovery? It takes focus and a desire to be free from suffering. However, it is a path open to all. I will walk you through what I have rediscovered on my journey back to the space of presence within.

At the end of the book, the mindfulness and meditation section will assist you on your journey with suggestions to help build a daily practice alongside your reading—if you so choose.

Questions to answer within each chapter are optional and intended for exploration to expand your awareness. Thus, you may not immediately see the connection of these questions with your reading. Nonetheless, these are poised to deepen your understanding when experienced through deep thought, meditative enquiry, or, if you so wish, in discussion with like-minded friends and loved ones. Purposeful change comes from presence with patience and with practice.

Now is your opportunity for

awe-inspiring change.

Be still

Rediscover The Creator Within

three

Presence & the ego

Change in the world happens
one thought at a time.
Change in us happens one thought at a time
and the most significant change,
with no thought at all.

Our gift as humans is our consciousness with which we create an experience beyond the physical world we explore via our senses. This personal reality is conjured in our imagination and stored in layers of memories, thoughts, and emotions that, at times, obscure our natural state. These thoughts, comprised of our experience, we will call 'The Ego'.

In time we dream of a new layer of existence, experienced only by ourselves. This version of reality is not real in any physical sense other than the chemicals and sensations our bodies produce to support our self-told stories. It is entirely normal for individuals to become lost in the mind's recesses, rather than living completely focused and with purpose at this moment. We will look at this concept in detail as we progress.

The formation of the ego starts as soon as we are born (possibly, in utero). Initially, there can be no internal commentary. As babies, our basic needs for food and comfort are met by our carers when we cry; hence repetitive behaviour creates our expectations.

Learned labels help us as a child to communicate and navigate the world. A bird 'just is' something to be observed until we understand that others know the object of attention as 'a bird'. We then store an inner commentary for future use. More things take on labels; trees, pretty flowers, a rose, a bumblebee as time passes. These concepts become more than learned language, as we add preferences of what should and should not be happening in our experience. The bee stings! Bees create pain and may be feared. The parent is affirmed (or not) as a being of safety, love, and comfort as they soothe, and a new story and expectation are retained as truth.

In similar future events, the script is played out in our minds to prepare us for likely outcomes. When the stored version is at odds with reality, we may react with fear, confusion, or anger. These negative emotions may persist even throughout our adult years. With each new label and expectation, we can step away from our natural blissful state. We become powerfully identified with our thoughts and assumptions rather than experiencing what is before us now in real-time.

Over time, our perceptions of reality can become massively distorted, based entirely on and deeply identified with our own experience. Many people spend months or even years feeling depressed when life unfolds at odds with their expectations. So much energy is spent resisting change and wishing things were different. We rarely notice the choice to remain in an uncomfortable status quo as precisely that, a choice.

Unhappiness arises from not understanding how to see and accept the reality around us as it is. The strong association with our internal narrative can lead us to forget that every person has a unique view of life, resulting in internal conflict or disputes with those around us. No two people can see life identically. Every experience offers a unique perspective at a particular point in time, sometimes experienced by others diametrically opposite to our own yet equally 'real' and valid.

Only the ego's constructs, our self-told stories, make life appear personal. The more we step out of the stories we tell ourselves, the deeper we emerge in the present moment and vice versa. When in a healthy body and mind, our ego program will continue to run. Our minds are designed to chatter to make sense of our experience and keep us safe. For those of you who meditate, this is an important concept to consider.

Through self-enquiry, we can come to understand our stories, their meaning, and where their value lies. When we live in awareness of our thinking (noticing it) rather than giving attention to this internal dialogue, our thoughts soothe in meditative stillness.

There are many different interpretations of the ego. To avoid confusion, this is the definition we will be using:

Ego

The persona an individual adopts
made up of personal thoughts,
self-generated labels
and expectation born of experience.

A thought-form derived from
an individual's experiences.

Presence comes from the word 'present', meaning to exist here, now; to be focused on, or involved in, what you are doing or experiencing. Thus, presence is the state of existing, occurring, or being present in a particular place in this moment. It is also someone or something that cannot be seen but of which you are aware.

Throughout this book, I will use the word presence, meaning the force that runs through you and me. It is a feeling of bliss, love, awe, and completeness, the natural state of every human waiting to be rediscovered.

Presence is the 'factory reset' state of existence, in which only the true self or the true 'I am' remains, a boundless energy field of possibilities waiting to be directed. The quiet voice of intuition and the sixth sense become louder in presence and synchronicities more frequent and noticeable.

With a calm and present mind,
we access the space of creation within us
for the conscious direction
of any personal world we choose,
composed of love, bliss and harmony.

Without fully understanding how, some people find themselves in presence, typically through hardship and life challenges. Others find their way to self-discovery through the path of introspection. We can liken rediscovering presence to falling in love, boom! You are all in love at first sight or find yourself falling gradually, letting go as you learn about yourselves, trusting all is and will be well. We develop an awareness of the thoughts that lead us away from our true nature, integrating simple practices that keep us from attending to our worrying minds. Either way, in becoming self-aware, we live deeper in presence.

There are levels of presence to be experienced with so many entry points that pass us by daily. In musing over the following, be kind and honest with yourself. I suspect if we wish to live a life more fully present, we all have work to do:

- How often do you engage with your phone rather than being attentive to a friend or loved one in the same room?
- On your average day, when walking or completing everyday tasks, how lost in thought are you?

- In conversation, how engaged and present are you with your children, partner or friends?

N.B. Your ego will dictate interest in and how you engage with what is happening around you. These preferences are different and separate from the awareness of this moment.

Steps to presence and a still mind can be subtle shifts. For example, being focused on the task at hand or using our senses to become intensely aware of everything around us are each a step back to presence. The simplicity of making eye contact with the person you communicate with pulls your focus literally to this moment. In the practice of deep listening, our focus is entirely on the speakers' words and demeanour. When we detach from our internal commentary regarding their words, we create space to hear their story wholeheartedly. The upshot is that we are then free to respond without personal preference or empty agreement. This focus entirely on the present is sometimes referred to as 'losing the ego'.

More simple day-to-day practices to help you move towards a life lived deeper in presence are listed under the mindfulness and meditation section at the end of this book. Each of them provides opportunities to reconnect with the space of calm within us.

In becoming aware of our experience as each moment arises, we practice a living meditation that brings our existence to a new aliveness. Thus, space is created for 'true' thought pertinent to now, rather than concocted from stories born of experience or hopes and fears of an unreal future.

Awareness in this moment is entirely and eternally where our power lies.

In presence

In presence, the power of thought is fulfilled
as the fabrications of the mind melt away.
Self-given labels and thoughts that would historically
have brought great suffering
can be seen with amusement.

We are not our thoughts.
We are the awareness of our thoughts!

When resting in presence,
we embrace the past, present, and future,
observing the impersonal nature of 13.8 billion years of
creation eternally conceiving and supporting life.

Everything has led entirely to now,
providing all things necessary to sustain life.

With the integration of this realisation,
there comes an acceptance that everything "just is",
accompanied by a tremendous sense of love,
awe and gratitude for all things.

All fear and judgement fall away,
and we welcome our future created by thought
with curiosity and eagerness
in the understanding
we are indeed the scribes of our own experience.

Beyond the ego to presence:

- The ego is a thought-form derived from our personal experiences.
- Our ego evolves and can often obscure our natural state of calm.
- Every person experiences life from a unique perspective. All experience and resultant thoughts and feelings are equally valid.
- We create our experience of our life through our senses and in imagination. Our bodies support our stories producing chemicals (happy, angry, sad, sexual, etc.) augmenting reality by creating habitable experiences (conversely, it could occasionally be argued to develop uninhabitable experiences).
- Life does not happen to us. Life unfolds, and we decide how to feel about it.
- Presence is the 'factory reset' state of existence, in which everything we are or ever perceive arises.

- We can experience presence in many layers, e.g.:
  - When we connect to our intuition.
  - When we are so involved in a moment or task, we are in the flow of things, unaware of anything else, without noticing time passing.
  - When we abandon thoughts of past and future and the mind is calm at the moment. For example, coming literally to your senses to be aware of what is around you now, what you hear, smell, feel, etc. and experiencing all you sense as if for the first time, with no commentary.
  - Without a thought, in a state of bliss, love, awe, and completeness.

Q What is the difference between awareness of our thinking and attending to our thoughts?

You are an energy field of possibilities

You are an energy field of possibilities

waiting to be directed.

Wherever you start today,

you can become whomever you choose.

You are the creator of your reality.

Presence & the ego

Rediscover The Creator Within

four

Words for courage

There are times and events in life that can elicit tremendous uncertainty, fear and suffering. On the journey of overcoming our fears and moving into a place of peace about life's happenings, there will likely be times when we are drawn back into the drama of our minds.

The following words are a reference to help soothe and guide you during challenging times:

Dear one

Within you is a place of peace, strength, and wisdom
waiting for you to ask for help and guidance.
You know your suffering and
when the time is right for it to stop.

Have patience and trust that
all you wish for is waiting for you.

Focus your mind on how you want to feel.
Imagine yourself full of love and life in that feeling.
How you will get there is not your concern.
A path will open up to you at the right time.

It may hurt, seeming so far away.
It may make you weep.
Stay true to the feeling by carrying it with you.
All good things are possible for YOU.

Change by doing something different today.
When you wake, count 3,2,1, and get out of bed.
Left foot, right foot, shower,
get dressed and feed yourself.
Move more today than you did yesterday.

Take time to feel gratitude for
the good things in your life.
Be the source of love and kindness
for someone else.

Have trust.
Have patience.
Today is a new day.

Today you can choose to start the journey
into a life that you were born to live.

Rediscover The Creator Within

five

Knowing you know nothing is

the way to a breakthrough

Y ou are more than the sum of your biology and your experiences. You are more than the person you perceive yourself to be. You are expansive when you let go of what you already *think* you know and feel each thought and experience anew.

In essence, although vastly oversimplified in explanation, our aim is to learn to see and experience everything as if for the first time, without judgement, with child-like excitement and curiosity.

You are the no-thing from which something arises.

Q You are the no-thing from which something arises. What does this mean?

Rediscover The Creator Within

six

What is thought?

A large part of the human role is to learn how to use our
experience of thought to stabilise the entropy
(the declining harmony) of our minds,
balancing chaos with stillness
for good health and longevity.

Perhaps now is an excellent juncture to consider in more detail the purpose of thought. Although going back to basics may feel like elementary logic, what we believe we already know is often our stumbling block to growth.

Our thought is the process by which we relate to the external world, the primary function appearing to be survival, self-preservation, and procreation. In early human history, when we lived in small tribes, thought was pretty simple:

- Assess danger.
- Find the best methods of fulfilling primary needs.
- Nurture a position within the tribe to ensure cooperation for health and wellbeing.

The most successful did and still do so, with reasoning, logic, and good communication, all thought projections.

The tribe of the human race is now vast, with many cultures within cultures. Each has a myriad of collective consciousness influencing our thoughts. Global rules of right and wrong, 'do no harm', are hard-wired in our subconscious, needing little thought day by day, and legal systems, therefore, emphasise the ability to think about the consequence of our actions.

Less obvious 'rules', for example, table manners or permissible language, vary from family to family, even person to person within a family. So who and what is 'right'? Ensuring a place of total peace and security whilst fulfilling our growing list of superficial needs is so complicated that our minds struggle to keep up and disharmony is often the result.

Thought

The primary purpose of thought
is to 'record' experience for the
survival of the individual and species and
for internal and external harmony for longevity.

We all learn at our level of consciousness based on our experiences, and we cannot know that which is beyond our reality. For example, a child has no way of understanding all the complex rules that their senior relatives have become accustomed to over a lifetime. What could we fully comprehend of others' lives when they are so culturally and experientially different to our own? What could we know of life beyond our Universe with no frame of reference?

We think, make choices and act based on our learning level, from our point of view. The result? No person can ever please all people, all the time. We can try to understand someone else's perspective, yet we can only comprehend within the framework of our life experience.

With anxiety and depression running at such high levels globally, perhaps now is the time to notice, understand and harness our thinking? Is it time to recognise that we all do our best within the confines of our experience, that we are ALL always 'enough'?

When humans do not interfere with the world's natural balance, our basic needs, food, drink, shelter, sleep, and oxygen, are met daily. Nature provides so effortlessly that we have created a new layer of 'needs' and feel hard done by when they are not met. Look at the size of the Universe and ponder for one moment the commonly held thought that our life should unfold as we wish, that our lives should be different, that we should have more. Is this desire for control not amusing in its child-like naiveté? So many of us struggle to pat our heads and rub our stomachs in circles simultaneously. Thank goodness none of us is responsible for setting the orbits of the planets and providing for the needs of all creatures while keeping our heart beating, blood circulating and remembering to breathe!

Only our ego programs lead to our expectations of the world and how we are 'supposed' to experience it. Yet, all is as it should be, creation evolving, supporting and sustaining life.

Everything is as it should be

Life unfolds for us to experience.
Only our minds tell us things should be different.
So the subconscious and unseen forces
work for our survival.
Everything is as it should be, maintaining life
as creation unfolds in a perfectly balanced order.

Subconscious & conscious mind

Subconscious mind: if we think of the brain as a computer, the subconscious mind is the hard drive, recording everything we experience. Can we perhaps go further in saying it transfers information to and from the cloud? This data serves as a blueprint directing behaviour in patterns commensurate with our unique programming. As the primary function appears to be survival and longevity, it works to keep us within our comfort zones in our everyday behaviour habits. Its design makes us feel uncomfortable when we step outside recorded parameters in thought or deed. This programming is why so many of us find change challenging. Our 'hard drive' can be accessed consciously yet more often runs on auto-pilot. It also responds and is programmed/reprogrammed via conscious commands.

The autonomic nervous system regulates the body in optimal functioning condition and works in the most part subconsciously. It is responsible for the fight or flight response and sexual arousal and relies on stimulus from the conscious, present mind. We need the subconscious for so many reasons. It is impossible to be consciously present 100% of the time.

Conscious mind: Awareness of existence, thoughts, and sensations of the surrounding environment in this present moment.

We experience everything in the following ways:
- Through the five senses.
- From images and feelings derived from experience (Ego).
- From what lies beyond our thoughts in presence. (For those of you who meditate, I invite you to investigate this space further.)

Thoughts and actions can arise from our experience without our conscious involvement, to the extent that we do not know what we will say or do until we take action. Scientific brain scans can predict a subject's next decision 4 to 11 seconds before they are even aware of making them! The brain trawls stored records making decisions, and we become aware of our actions as they happen. Drunken amnesia, sleep-walking, driving, and suddenly being aware of where you are, are all examples of the subconscious's power.

A fun way to witness the body on auto-pilot is to imagine taking a large bite from a juicy lemon. See yourself putting the lemon to your mouth and notice what happens as you bite down and swish the juice around. What do you experience? If this doesn't work for you, take a moment to refocus and replace the lemon's image with something you would find repulsive, and then note your reaction!

Even though we imagined the lemon in this instance, our bodies run stored programs built from experience, releasing an immediate physical response. Next time you feel a physical reaction or an emotion and do not know what has triggered it, remind yourself that the body is continually running programs exploring your experience. Our hormones can, for example, make us feel sad for a short time for no particular reason, and that is OK. We do not always need to heed our emotions or look for a related story to give them merit.

**Sometimes, it is enough to become aware of the
emotion and wait patiently as it passes,
noticing how it feels in your body.**

A moment of present mindfulness (for example, taking a deep breath and relaxing from top to toe whilst counting back from five to one) can be grounding. This stillness brings focus to this moment's reality, shaking off unwanted feelings and stifling the fuel of emotion— thought.

We can, and do, create and build any feeling or emotion when we attach an appropriate memory.

If you try to feel angry, what do you notice?

Emotions do not exist for more than a moment in isolation. We must feed them with our thoughts to bring them to life. Good memories are lovely and release hormones beneficial to our health when recalled. You can use them as an anchor to elicit a good feeling when you need a boost. Bring to mind thoughts of a pet, person or place you love that fills you with a pleasant feeling. When you close your eyes and slow your breath, bask in those feelings. As the positivity washes over, you are returned to a calm body and mind, restoring harmony and balance.

By noticing the feelings that arise as you focus on a joyful moment, you create an easily accessible anchor to summon when your thoughts wander back to challenging events you are not yet ready to face.

Our auto-pilot mode is the state in which many of us exist and perform everyday tasks. We carry on conversations with little conscious, present awareness; each thought and action rolls into the next commensurate with and predetermined by our programming. We say and do what a lifetime of experience has brought us to based on our exclusive, imagined truth.

Is it starting to become clear why there is no choice when living life in the subconscious's auto-pilot mode? Remember, universal laws of right and wrong, particularly do no harm, are hard-wired in our subconscious and guide us daily.

We can and do only apportion blame without conscious, present thought. In presence, there is no judgment on ourselves or others for our thoughts and actions.

A decision made in a moment
cannot hold judgement,
other than in retrospect
or from a different personal perspective.

Life isn't personal, fair or unfair; everything 'just is as it is'. Thoughts such as 'should have done/should have been' are therefore foolish and lead to disharmony. Noticing when you use the word 'should' and dropping the story behind your thinking is empowering. You or they behaved in a certain way because it was proportional to the level of life experience at that moment in time.

Letting go of our stories built up in ego and becoming consciously present leads us to step out of our drama and into a life of bliss, love, and joy.

A note of caution. In becoming aware we are not our thoughts, a new layer of thinking will often take its place. Taking responsibility for all our emotions can lead to self-judgement. Remember, a desire to change the past is borne only from new experiences post that moment. This new perspective can give direction on how we 'should' have behaved. Gracious acceptance of our past actions will prevent the mind from spiralling.

There is no good or bad, right or wrong, only how we perceive things to be, at this point in time. We are complete, enough, and we add positive energy to the world when we work with what life offers.

Exercise examples:

The blame game–'Should' example:

Choose a time frame between two to seven days, during which you fully commit to noticing each instance when you judge yourself and others using 'should' and 'why'. Next, write down the judgments you make when you catch yourself saying or thinking the words 'should' or 'why'. Then, using your learning, how can you make sense of the situation?

When I used a blaming word:
The other morning I felt an agitation building. Whenever thoughts flowed for this book, one of my daughters would appear for a hug or attention. I felt agitation mixed with frustration and guilt as I 'should' be more attentive as a mother.

What was the result of portioning blame?:
I felt agitation, frustration and feelings of inadequacy. My thinking spiralled to the negative.

Question the validity of your thoughts. What is true?:

In questioning why a beautiful hug from my girls was causing negative emotions, I understood that not being freely available was at odds with a big part of the label I have given myself, aka 'Mummy' and how I perceive my role.

The next step was to question the validity of my thinking.

Was it true that I was not available to my girls? No. I have chosen to give myself wholly to motherhood. Now I enter a new chapter, choosing to rediscover myself and, on the way, I will become a better Mum. In the future, I will give guidelines as to when I am working and when I am freely accessible. Internal peace and harmony were restored, creating an environment in which we three girls thrive.

N.B. This solution was the result of my thinking. Your thought patterns may be very different, leading you to your unique resolve in a similar situation. The key is to notice and challenge your feelings of guilt to dissolve negative emotions without judging yourself or others.

The blame game–"Why" Example:

When I used a blaming word:

Chocolate Pretzels called my name. I don't even love them, but in times of stress, sugar is so tempting. Delicious if you eat just the right amount, yet without good thought, I munched my way through a whole bag. The fault-finder in my head was on form; "Why did you do that? You really shouldn't have!"

What was the result of portioning blame?:

These self-deprecating thoughts started a negative spiral of bad feelings. Not yet finished, my internal judgemental voice pipes up, "You have had weight problems all your life. You won't choose to eat consciously!" My feelings dropped even lower.

Question the validity of your thoughts. What is true?:

What is true is that for much of my life, I have eaten with little thought. Now I understand that the negative feelings are taking me away from good health, longevity, and my journey to be present. I can choose to eat to nourish and support my body. By understanding what my guilt is telling me, I take back my power.

Will you choose to notice when you apportion blame? It is easier to continue within comfort zones in the short term. Your subconscious will give you many reasons to stay as you are and resist putting pen to paper to complete the blame game exercise. We move away from our most significant pain. Change challenges our norm, bringing discomfort, yet the thought of change is often more challenging than the shift itself. Do you want to remain in familiar ways or to experience expansive growth and change?

Exercise:

The blame game

Choose a time frame over the next two to seven days during which you commit to noticing how you judge yourself and others using the words 'Should' and 'Why'.

When I used the blaming word:

_____

_____

_____

What was the result of apportioning blame?:

_____

_____

_____

Question the validity of your thoughts. What is true?
(Tip: reality will always make us feel loving, calm, neutral, and in the flow of life):

_____

_____

_____

_____

_____

_____

_____

Harnessing thought:

- When we recognise our stories and understand our thoughts, feelings, and emotions, we step out of suffering and towards presence. Is it your time to become aware of the perfection of all things?

- The primary purpose of thought is to 'record' experience for the survival of the individual and species for internal and external harmony and longevity. Ego, logic, reasoning, and communication are projections of thought.

- We all learn at our level of consciousness based on the experiences we live. We also only comprehend within the framework of our life experience.

- Our basic needs, food, drink, sleep, and oxygen, are met daily when our environment is in its natural order.

- Thoughts, emotions, and their projections can arise unsolicited. We do not have to look for a related story. We can recognise a thought or feel an emotion and let it pass by focusing on how it feels in the body.

- We must 'feed' emotions to keep them alive.

- All suffering is the result of how we use our thoughts, subconscious or conscious. Unhappiness comes from not accepting reality as it is.
- Thinking life or people should be different is foolishness.
- There is no judgement other than from a place of ego.

Q Have you noticed how on some days, for example, someone dancing and singing in delight can fill you with joy, and the same event on a different day can cause such irritation? What is different?

Q Our brain interprets our sensory experience. Can we ever experience anything outside the body? What might this mean?

Rediscover The Creator Within

seven

Lift your mood

We are supposed to feel negative emotions at times as a compass to keep us safe and get back into life's flow, but not for too long. So if you notice your energy is slipping or is well and truly on the way to rock bottom, this is a handy "pick 'n mix" to try out:

1. Turn up the corners of your mouth for as long as you can in a forced smile.

2. Take a long breath in through your nose. Tip your head back and blow out all the air in your lungs whilst at the same time turning up the corners of your mouth.

3. Move your body more than you usually do. Motion creates energy and helps invite flow into your life.

4. Get out into nature and sunlight.

5. Go for a walk.

6. Exercise is known to release positive chemicals to help your mood. Exercise doing something you enjoy.

7. Drink plenty of water to nourish and cleanse your body.

8. Eat a balanced diet to nourish your body and balance hormones.

9. Practice temperance in all; in food, drink and exercise for the right balance of body and mind.

10. Come off social media and other people's highlight reels.

11. Move away from screens and engage with the real world.

12. Get regular sleep. Too little can render us tired and less able to focus. Too much sleep in the daytime could lead to your body balance falling out of sync and leave you needing to sleep all the time.

13. Hug a friend, loved one, or a pet.

14. Connect with people, especially those you admire. Quality relationships are the key to good health.

15. Engage in chit chat with people you meet. Smile and make eye contact.

16. Think of something that fills you with uncomplicated love, such as a pet, child or a favourite place.

17. Pursue a hobby that excites you.

18. Watch a film to make you laugh.

19. Listen to uplifting music.

20. Dance–the sillier, the better. If you don't dance, shake it out!

21. Inhale a pleasing scent such as orange or lavender.

22. Breath in, tensing your shoulders. Breath out and release the tension. Tap your right shoulder with your left hand, and then your right shoulder with your left hand.

23. Declutter.

24. Break tasks down into manageable sized chunks. Focus on one thing at a time.

25. Help others.

26. Be the source. If you need compassion, be compassionate to someone who needs it more. If you need friends, be a friend, etc.

27. Do something nice for someone.

28. Practice positive self talk. What are you good at doing? Start with 1–3 things that make you feel alive.

_____

_____

_____

29. Practice gratitude. Name 1–3 things you are grateful for.

_____

_____

_____

30. Practice mindfulness (see the mindfulness and meditation section).

31. Practice meditation.

32. Notice negative thoughts. Write them down and challenge their validity.

33. Try energy tapping. With your middle three fingers, tap:

- Between the eyebrows
- Along your cheekbones
- Chin
- Collar bones
- Down along the sternum
- Ribs
- Knees
- Ankle bones

34. Work with a Life Coach.

Ask for professional help if you need it.

Q What other things will help YOU?

Rediscover The Creator Within

eight

The past exists in memory

Now is all there is, this point in time
that creates, directs, and affects our future.

So few of us invest our energy fully in this moment. The past has gone, and the future remains a dream. All we can affect is here at this moment.

Introspection and curiosity are positive when used for self-exploration to keep us moving forward positively. For instance, if a person falls off a horse, they can choose to spend the rest of their lives being afraid of horses, or they can get back on and enjoy the ride. How we use energy from our experiences is our choice to make.

It would be detrimental to our chances of surviving and thriving if we moved into total amnesia about the past. Positive memories are helpful when we use them as anchors to elicit good feelings, provided we don't get lost in them, wishing things were now as they used to be. When we lose loved ones, we carry the love we shared throughout life, and that love never leaves us.

Risk assessment is a crucial life skill and is positive when used in good measure at the appropriate time. Yet, the genes passed on by our cautious ancestors can be overplayed, particularly when life is or has been challenging. Let me illustrate in a silly example. A group of cavemen pop their heads out into the world. One is immediately pounced upon and gobbled up by a bloodthirsty predator. The following day the survivors leave the cave. Those with gruesome memories running through their minds exercise caution with their fight, flight, or freeze program on high alert. The others rush out, their minds on food and wallop! A hungry predator gobbles them up. Those with the cautious trait live to pass on learning and their genes.

It has become our nature to be wary. Negative thoughts, feelings, and emotions are an essential part of our survival instinct. Worry in the 'right' moment is good when heeded, and action is taken. In the modern world, where threats are more diverse than those faced by our early ancestors, our physical and mental health and longevity depend upon the understanding, use, and direction of our feelings and emotions. No living body is designed to function at a high level of stress for a long time. The zebra receives a burst of energy as it flees a predator in survival mode. Its instincts and motion become activated as nature intended. Once the threat is over, the zebra returns to its natural calm state, grazing in the grass, balance restored.

Our human brain cannot distinguish between real and imagined threats. So, unwittingly, we repeatedly re-live simulated scenarios. In reviewing an experience in mind, feelings are recalled, resulting in real-time hormone release. These chemicals bring life and energy to our memories.

Our world can spiral as negative feelings and emotions lead to more negative thoughts. Attention to our thoughts results in feelings; feelings become emotions, and our perceived reality is created in body and mind. In the actual situation we find ourselves reviewing, the resultant hormones would have been to our advantage. However, in our mind-made simulation, they are rarely of benefit and can become harmful over time. This redundant, natural chemical waste produced by our bodies can lead to poor health if we become stuck in a repeating loop of negativity.

Rumination, going over and over events in our mind, is self-induced emotional and physical suffering.

Many of us brood negatively over the past to some degree. Do you identify with the following list of everyday worries?

- Stewing over small matters.
- Ruminating on disagreements.
- Fretting over lost sleep.
- Worrying over money spent.
- Self-loathing after over indulgences.
- Regretting the lack of exercise.
- Anxiety about work issues.
- Obsessing about time management.
- Frustration over a house left unclean.
- Worry about relationships.

Conversations that have gone wrong, mistakes made, love lost, abuse, if not in this moment, can no longer cause distress–unless we enliven the memory. Instead, WE add this drama to our lives. If left to run unchecked, these thoughts can build, leading to unhappiness or depression. Every unsettling thought is an emotional call to redirect attention and energy to the present moment. The past is gone and cannot be changed. Recognising that all is well now in real-time allows harmony and space for the constructive direction of our future.

Negative feelings are a call to action to change our situation to prevent a repeat of adverse events

or,

to change how we think about the past
for a peaceful mind and body.

As we have explored, memories do sometimes arrive uncalled. In noticing that it is thes images created in the mind that cause our suffering, we take the first step in loosening their grip. You hold the key to letting go of painful memories. Once again, you can confront your negative 'film strips' with courage and let them run, this time as an observer watching a movie. Images and feelings drift away as your lessons are understood, and the hold of the past diminishes.

The past can't hurt unless re-lived in memory.
There is only one person in charge of your thoughts.
That person is you.

- "But you don't understand what happened to me and how much it has damaged me."
- "But I was so mistreated."
- "But no one knows how much I am suffering and what I am dealing with."
- "But I don't know how to stop thinking about it."

Assuming there is no imminent danger at this moment, you are safe. Do you have fresh air to breathe? Do you have food and water if you are hungry or thirsty? Only our egos tell us things should be different from reality. We are rarely unable to bear what is happening at this moment when our mind is still enough to be in present awareness.

We have free will to choose how we think and feel about what life presents. Well-directed thoughts and feelings deliver all we wish for when we learn to harness their power.

In part, the secret to a happy, fulfilled life is to know which stories of the past serve us and which ones we can let go. Letting go of the past is a practice; we must rewire our brains towards different, more helpful thought patterns.

The peculiar truth is that the shift to presence takes focus yet no effort. When we learn how to interpret our past, stories that are no longer helpful fall away; life becomes harmonious and joyful to experience. Rediscovering the real you, is worth your consideration. You can train your brain to be attentive to this moment with minimal effort rather than becoming lost in old stories.

If we spend too long fighting memories and making them personal, this moment and all the gifts life has to offer are missed. Time moves forwards, and so must we.

We cannot miss our opportunity of entering presence. Rather, it is impossible to miss our chance to enter presence as our reality to experience is eternally here and now. So be patient, and know every moment we exist is an opportunity to embrace our creative, blissful space of existence.

All pain is a call to action. Life hurts sometimes but to stay in suffering is a choice. It is a choice to continue looking back or make a conscious decision to use empowering thought to create a better, more harmonious future.

Unfortunately, no person lives feeling happy 100% of the time, as many of us wish we could. Our feelings and emotions allow the gift of contrast for us to experience. So although seemingly inviting, a lifetime of 'vanilla' would be very dull and most likely short.

Live in the moment

There is only this moment.

When the mind sees 'now' is all there is,

space is made for clear thought.

Good conscious thought of heart, mind, and soul,

directing the creation of the personal world in love.

The present is where all power resides.

A space of innate omnipresent bliss,

Waiting to be rediscovered by you.

The past is but a memory:

- The past is gone; the future's not set. Now is the point in time that creates, directs, and affects our future.

- The past can only hurt if we give energy to our thoughts.

- In noticing and welcoming our thoughts, good or bad, we start to direct our thinking positively and guide our destiny with grace, at our will.

- Negative feelings are a call to action to redirect energy to prevent a repeat of the past or change how we think in the present.

- Negative thinking is often the route of less resistance—in the short term. Becoming optimistic takes work and intentional focus.

- Thinking happy thoughts can act as an anchor when the mind is in chaos.

- When we find ourselves complaining about our woes, we can take a moment to calm our thinking and question the validity of our thoughts by viewing them from a different perspective.
  - Centre yourself in this moment.
  - What memory is causing your distress?
  - Everything is as it is. The past could not have been different, and the future's not set.
  - What other perspectives can you witness?
- Intuition and well-directed thought combined symbiotically steer us in the direction of any future we choose.
- Our seemingly real mind and body made augmented reality fall away when we watch with awareness.
- The key to being in presence is to learn to live in this moment.

Rediscover The Creator Within

nine

All future is imagination

This moment is all there is, all we have control over, yet so many of us look to the future and worry about possible eventualities. Will the traffic be bad; will I get to work on time; what if I miss the bus; what if I mess up the presentation; what if I am not in for the parcel; have I enough phone battery; what is the right thing to wear; what if the weather is terrible. My stress levels are rising, just writing this list of everyday worries.

Worry, fear, and stress, overload our ability to solve problems, set goals, and complete tasks in the most efficient ways.

Around this mark, the mind will typically say, "I have to think of the future. How else can I make decisions!"

- "I have no job, and my family relies on me. I need to think about the future."
- "I may lose my job."

- "I don't have money to pay my bills. I will lose my house."
- "You don't know what is happening in my life."
- "I don't even know if I will live or die."
- "I am dying."

Excessive worrying about the future creates anxiety and clutters the mind, clouding out clear thought. When rational thought diminishes, we lose the ability to direct life to the good. Worry can become a habit and is exhausting, both physically and mentally.

So many problematic situations resolve themselves without our intervention. A tiny percentage of the things we worry about actually come to pass, and when they do, our experience is rarely as bad as we feared. Looking realistically at the probability of our fears coming to fruition can help us return to calm or, when necessary, prepare for the inevitable.

Following many tests, Doctors told Zane and Amara that they could not have children. Holding onto a dream, undeterred, they found an IVF clinic prepared to help. Amara recalls being excited to undergo treatment as it offered the possibility of making their dreams come true.

The process was an emotional roller coaster of hope and, when allowed, fear of what-ifs. One morning when Amara was not in the most positive frame of mind at the clinic, a nurse perceptively offered some advice. "Why be sad now? Will that make you feel any better in a few weeks if your treatment is unsuccessful?" Wise words that snapped her back to the present and positive thoughts about the fulfilment of their dream.

Will being sad and worried now make you feel any better in the future if your fears come to fruition?

Real crises bring out the best in people, and they find a strength they never knew they had. In Spring 2020, the UK was in lockdown due to Covid-19. At the outset of the global pandemic, people stayed home. They were only permitted outside their homes to shop for essentials, exercise, or perform critical worker roles to slow the disease's spread.

Mia lived in rented accommodation where, before lockdown, the Landlady gave notice for the family to vacate as she needed to sell. There were very few rental properties on the market, and fewer still offering viewings due to the pandemic. In addition to the world crisis and the looming loss of somewhere to live, Mia's husband had a heart attack and was in a coma for several days. Hospitals were not permitting visitors, staff were too busy to field phone calls, and friends were not allowed to visit.

Mia's inner wisdom told her to let go of what was happening at the hospital. There was nothing she could do to change the situation. With the support of friends, she made a list of what she had control over. Her husband had historically been the driving force for many family decisions, yet Mia rose to the challenge and booked viewings for rental homes and ensured she and her daughters had access to money for food. She was wiser, more resilient and more robust than she ever thought herself to be.

When there truly is something to worry about, inner wisdom and guidance kick in, pointing us to where we can affect change. After a crisis, when minds wander back, we must remind ourselves the time of stress has passed. If there is no critical threat at this moment, all is well.

If a situation is causing you distress or worry, can you do anything about it?

- If 'Yes' when the time is right, dare to move from worry to action. Trust your intuition and focus on one thing at a time until completion.
- If 'No', is now the time to change your thinking about your circumstances?

**Worry and anxiety are a call to action
to redirect energy in a situation or
to change your thinking.**

To change, we need to be brave and face our fears with logic and presence. It is essential to recognise that doing nothing to change is a choice. The choice to stay with what we know even if it is uncomfortable or damaging.

Is it not better to make choices from well-directed empowering thoughts rather than doing nothing from a paralysing fear of the unknown? Trust your intuition and take action when you know it is time to make a change. If your intuition leads you to remain as you are today, what plans can you make for changes in your future?

Have you noticed how easy it is to see the solution to someone else's problem? From the outside, without all the mind chatter and emotion, it is clear that there is no big hurdle to overcome, but a series of smaller ones needing attention to reach calm waters.

Marie followed her sister into sales at a well-known company. Enticed by the success and acclaim her sister had and being sure of her worth, she too secured a position and, for many years, also enjoyed recognition and high rewards. As time passed, the company lost market share as the world around it changed. Marie found herself functioning on auto-pilot and complained that she was living in stress as her workload increased and pay fell. She wished she could find another position but was too overwhelmed by her business workload and bills at home. One day there was an internal email announcing redundancies in the sales team. Marie became even more distressed, fearing her financial security was about to be taken away. With such anxiety built up over many years, it was difficult to logically see the situation's truth. She was a top-performing salesperson, and her position would not be under threat. Even if the company were to fold, she could sell her way into a new job, or even better, she could use the opportunity to take redundancy and find a new career.

In a short time, her thinking focused on the positive. She left behind fearful thoughts of being without a job or money to support her family. Being unready to give control to fate, she used the experience as a spur to take positive action to secure a new position whilst keeping her own. Within a few days, she had been offered two new jobs in addition to her own. Her energy levels lifted. For the first time in many years, she was excited about her opportunities.

When thoughts and feelings are focused on the positive, a clear path opens up to the future with anxiety falling away. Ask yourself, is your thinking based on fact or based on fear?

Challenge yourself, remembering only a tiny percentage of the things we worry about actually happen. Re-harness all energy used for worry and put it to better use.

When we plan for the future in presence,
with a calm mind,
the flow of life directs us with positive energy
to a life that feels inviting.

Worry creates and demands energy. We can harness this energy and turn it to the positive. When our minds wander to a future where we have no control, we have options open to us. We can use hormone release by putting our bodies in motion, for example going for a walk, exercising, gardening, cleaning the house or dancing. These activities put energy to work, and as the stress leaves the body, it is replaced by good feelings.

Following this movement with a mindfulness exercise, such as listening to music or bird song, taking a few deep, slow breaths, will help ground you, bringing you to a calm presence.

When faced with illness or the end of life, it can be challenging to change our thoughts about what can feel like such a devastating time. Life can become all about our diagnosis, hospital visits and a fear of what is ahead. It takes presence, bringing ourselves here, now to this moment, to take back our power. Therein we embody an innate knowledge, knowing that resistance takes us away from the peace within us. When we cannot change our situation, there is forever one thing we have power over, our thoughts. Fighting for life with awareness in the present moment can bring great courage and acceptance of what is, whilst enjoying the experiences and gifts life yet has to offer.

I am fortunate enough to work with Marie Curie as a nominated friend for people who have a terminal diagnosis. I visited dearest Mary for the last time before she gained her wings. She smiled as she took my hand, and we recalled some of the beautiful things we had done in our time together. One of my fondest memories was of a day we sat outside a coffee shop. She was too sick to eat the tiny taster of cake, so she slowly fed it to the birds. Such a simple experience filled her with great joy, firmly focused in her present, watching the sparrows chirp and scrap for every crumb. We pinned lavender to her collar, and Mary savoured the beautiful bouquet. She lived every moment that day. As long as we have breath, there is beauty in this world for us to enjoy.

There was so much good that came into Mary's life in her final months. She saw family members not visited for years. Old rifts no longer carried meaning, and she spent her last days with her dear daughter after realising "we fell out over nothing really". Family and friends gave precious time to drop by and take her on short trips. She was showered with more love in the last months of her life than she knew was available to her. Even grief at losing her dearest husband of 60 years returned to love, feeling she would be with him again soon.

No person needs to live in sadness, fear, loneliness or anxiety. This moment as we experience it in real-time, is so infrequently unbearable. Life is here to be lived and offers many gifts when we are still enough to recognise and receive them. Looking for what we have to be grateful for is hard at times, yet there is always good when we take time to be still. Life will play out around us; we do not need to lose ourselves in its drama.

In presence, there is sadness at a loss of a loved one. Yet, as the waves of remembering wash over, the heartaches and feelings are known as love. Memories can still bring tears whilst accepting that the cherished loved one was a gift for a time.

All too often, we try to resist life as it unfolds. Many of us waste energy dwelling in the negative. Resistance is futile! Life changes, life evolves, life and death happen. All of our feelings and emotions, positive and negative, play a role in how we acclimatise. Anxiety and depression are nipped in the bud when we consciously direct our feelings, thoughts and emotions. With diligent awareness of our mood changes, we reduce time spent lost in stories by challenging their validity and stop downward spirals at their source.

Being in presence at this moment is powerful, putting us in our innate space of peace, bliss and joy. Therein lies an acceptance that all things are as they are, knowing that fighting 'what is' would lead to our suffering. Living fully in each moment as it presents offers the opportunity for deep peace and acceptance of what is yet to come.

Don't worry, be happy:

- This moment is all there is, all we have control over.
- So many problematic situations resolve themselves without our intervention.
- Question if your worries are based on fact or in fear. What is the actual probability of your worst fears coming to fruition?
- Will being sad and worried now make you feel any better in the future if your fears do come to fruition?
- In a crisis, people follow their intuition.
- Focus on the present to be clear of mind.
  - If a situation is causing you distress or worry, can you do anything about it?
  - If Yes, dare to move from worry to action.
  - If No, is it time to change your thinking?
- Doing nothing to change is a choice.
- Prioritise. Tackle one task at a time to completion. Break each task into manageable pieces.
- Harness negative energy and use it physically, e.g. dance, garden, go for a walk.

- Return your mind to a place of calm and clear thought with a mindfulness exercise.
- Look to see the positives for which you can be grateful. Harness positive thinking to lead you fearlessly forward.

Q When we have assessed risk, does it serve us to go over all possible threats?

Q When your thoughts wander to the future, what two go-to methods can you employ to immediately re-centre your focus on the present moment? (Your tools must come out of your bag for them to be helpful).

Let curiosity be your guide

When we live in fear,

We miss all life's good bits.

There is nothing to obtain,

only experience.

Slow down, relax.

Let curiosity be your guide.

All future is imagination

Rediscover The Creator Within

ten

Change your thoughts
to change your reality

As a man thinks, so shall he be.

It is quite a miracle that we can think and witness our thoughts at the same time. The next step in evolution is perhaps to consciously understand our feelings and emotions and direct our thoughts, lives, and creations forward more positively. Perhaps feelings are a sense forgotten by many or a sense waiting for us to develop?

Have you seen the long term widower who has become sure he can't find happiness? The delighted shrieks of children laughing and playing hurt him, and he shouts for them to "Be quiet!". Their energy levels are so far apart that the children's natural state of joy causes thoughts of bitterness and anger in his life to deepen. He turns away all those that could give him comfort or help him find joy. He alone can free himself of his pain and loneliness. At his core is a place of bliss where all new beginnings are possible. Does he need to live in sadness, pain or loneliness? These are conditions he has added to his life through unguarded thinking that, over time, have become his character. Feelings of resentment towards what should and should not be, have created the world he now sees around him.

**Suffering occurs when we want things to be other than they are.
We add empowering energy to the world when we work with what life offers us.**

Little children have such a zest for a life unencumbered by negativity and worry. They laugh at the slightest thing, living in awe, curiosity and amazement, singing, dancing, running, creating things and loving nearly every moment. The innocence and magic of childhood slip away with a long list of things to do and a world of negative thoughts about what should and should not be. Adults become weighed down. Life can be so busy we forget to make time for fun and creation. Perhaps it is for us to rediscover the wondrous world little ones live in and be like little children?

All we have become is the result of our thoughts. Curmudgeonly or jolly; Happy or sad; Rich, poor; Fat, thin; Confident or timid; Frustrated or free. The thinking we allow to linger affects us and becomes us, or at least that is the appearance. We have thoughts and feelings but, we are not our thoughts and feelings.

Human biology dictates that outward circumstances influence our thoughts. If a wild animal appears, we are wired to take immediate action for survival. Thinking creates feelings for a purpose, and at this juncture, if time allows, we must decide what they are telling us.

Too often, we run on the predetermined patterns of the subconscious without conscious thought of their effect. Our option is to learn to become aware of our emotions, good and bad and use them to direct our life to our will.

Familiarity with raw emotions, joy, trust, fear, surprise, sadness, anticipation, anger and disgust, and how each feels in our bodies can halt wandering thoughts before they become problematic or allow celebration at being in the flow of life.

The Robert Plutchik wheel of emotion diagram is an aid to help name some of our emotions. The outer petals are generally regarded as less intense energies than those in the centre of the wheel. When we recognise emotions as energy within our bodies, we can prevent the negatives from escalating whilst savouring the positives.

Next time you feel an emotion rising, stop and challenge yourself to see what you are experiencing and where you feel it in your body. You have now stepped into the world of becoming the observer of thought and can release emotion if unwarranted or disadvantageous at this moment. In doing so, you release tension in the body or embrace and savour the moment in positive emotion. Understanding emotions allows their use as intended for the good of our physical and mental health and longevity.

Exercise: Identifying Emotion

Robert Plutchik wheel of emotion:

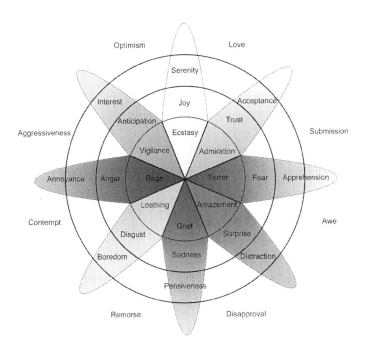

What emotion am I feeling?

_____

How does it feel in my body?

_____

Life is a rollercoaster:

- Thoughts become feelings, and feelings become emotions. If left unchecked, emotions eventually become integrated as personality traits and, in time, become our character.

- All feelings and emotions are essential, both positive and negative.

- Becoming intimately familiar with how emotions feel in our bodies can help stop negative feelings from becoming problematic.

- Consciously recognising and understanding our emotions allows us to move forward positively.

Q What does it mean 'to be as little children'?

Our nature is change

We find ourselves where all previous
events and thoughts have led us.
We are exactly who and where
we are supposed to be.

Be still.
Make no judgment.
Our nature is to change.

Follow your heart.
Work hard without effort.
Take time without the notice of time.

Step by step, small changes become us.
With our conscious will,
life is created at our direction.

Rediscover The Creator Within

eleven

Go with the flow of life

Flow is our creative state,
where the present is fully embraced.

When in the flow of life, we become lost in our experience, fully participating with pure, positive, creative energy.

Time evaporates as we lose ourselves in hobbies or life passions when we are 'in the zone'. In this state, there is no resistance, no desire to fight what life presents. We complete tasks with ease, often without thought or effort. Energy flows naturally, guiding us to act, or not, as the moment requires, without attachment to results and with a firm focus on what is before us now. When we are in a hurry or working on auto-pilot, our focus is attached to an outcome.

Swimming against the tide is exhausting. It is easy to become lost in a negative spiral of thought, leaving us on the rocks. When feeling disempowered, we must change direction in circumstance or thinking to put ourselves back in the flow of life.

A small gym was to merge with a much larger Health Club out of the blue. For many, this was unwelcome news and staff were left not knowing if they would have a job the following year. Amrit, a respected Physical Trainer, found the communication difficult. Until the onset of the merger, she had a passion for sport and passed it on as if it were the Olympic torch. However, her light dimmed when the gyms announced their merger. There was concern that some staff would not get a position in the new structure. Amrit was upset that she might not keep the job she so loved. Her negative thoughts manifested first as anger, which she soon started to voice, appearing to be 'anti company'. Depression followed with her continued resistance to the oncoming tide of change. When the newly formed Health Club announced the positions, Amrit was the only department member not to receive a job offer. From outside her story, we can perhaps see that her outcome would have likely been very different if she had worked with the changes.

Worry, stress, anxiety and depression can lead to bad decision-making and actions, compounding perceived problems. The idea that life sucks and cannot be improved is hence reinforced. Take time to check in with your thoughts as they will soon become feelings, and feelings are your superpower.

Feelings create your experience.

If your thoughts make you feel good, you are floating into your joy. If they are pulling you down, it is time to stop swimming against the tide!

What do you need to change? Your situation, thinking or both? Taking time to fix your emotions will lead you to your dreams, for you are more powerful than you know.

A new boss moved into a business. Jennifer, the head of finance, was adamantly against the change forced upon her and resolved to make life difficult for the new General Manager. She submitted reports late and incomplete, which made life challenging for management and herself. As a result, Jennifer gained a low reputation with senior management, and ultimately she was placed on disciplinary notice. It was not long before Jennifer found herself out of a job.

How different would the story have been if she had accepted what life had delivered and resolved to make a positive change and go with the flow? We cannot control the world around us, but we can control how we think about it and, in doing so, direct our destiny positively. The longer we allow ourselves to stay in negative thoughts, the more poor feelings we have. Low feelings lead to negative emotions. Emotions left to run without our conscious awareness eventually become our character, our persona, by which the outside world knows us. We do become aligned with the thoughts we allow to remain in our awareness.

Noticing when life feels stuck or challenging is essential, and seeing where our core values are not honoured is helpful. Small changes can make a big difference. If we catch negative feelings as they emerge, we can stop the swelling tide of negative emotions.

Daniel was unsuccessful in his application for promotion in a company where he had worked for many years. In his stead, senior management hired an external candidate. Every day Daniel would go home to his wife feeling tired, worn down and unappreciated at work, complaining that his new boss did not know what he was doing. Daniel marvelled at how the management could employ such an inefficient manager. Being convinced he knew the industry better, he became offhand and argumentative in business meetings. His energy levels dropped, feeling cheated out of 'his' role, and his thoughts about his world turned more negative. Unsurprisingly, the newcomer soon had enough of the adversarial relationship and let Daniel go.

When we observe from the outside, uninvolved in Daniel's internal emotions, it is easy for us to see what he could have done for good mental health and career progression. There is always a choice to change our situation or change our thoughts for harmony and flow when change is not an option. The resistance to inevitable change serves no purpose and is tiring. Noticing and working with our feelings is the way to happiness and success.

The more mistakes we make, the wiser we become. We indeed become wiser with each mistake IF we take the time to understand what our feelings are telling us. It is

OK to feel negative emotions, such as anger, stress or anxiety, for short periods. These emotions serve as our compass and point out when we are moving against the flow of life.

Understanding what emotions mean allows space to redirect thinking and actions. When we interpret our emotions, the body quickly returns to a neutral state where energy flows freely, and stress responses stand down. If life feels like hard work, we are swimming against the tide.

It is OK to feel anger, stress or anxiety
for a short time.
Emotions are our compass,
pointing to the flow of life.

Life moves in constant change. The way to good health and a clear mind is to flow with it. Life is here for us to experience in its entirety, the whole gambit through good and bad. If it isn't possible to change something we desperately want to, we can convert the energy of resistance to positive action.

When feeling depressed or in need of compassion, it can be difficult for us to get out from under the duvet some days, let alone think of anyone else. Our pain can often feel like an immense burden and make us believe that everyone is happy and that no one can understand our situation. However, when we are clear of mind, is it not evident that there is always someone who needs help more than ourselves? When we become the source of what we feel is lacking in our lives, we are lifted out of the raging torrent to catch our breath.

In giving to those who need compassion, we can find purpose and balance. Offering love and care gives us reason to get up and face the day, knowing we are positively contributing to the world. It helps us to recognise that we have value. These symbiotic relationships become perfectly balanced, everyone gaining.

When you can't help yourself, be the light for others. In grief, give love to those around you. If feeling poor, become the source of wealth. Be the helping hand to someone below you when beaten down in your career. Giving produces so many positives within the body and acts as a conduit for more humanitarianism by those you touch in a positive and loving butterfly effect.

Where are you trying to swim against the flow of life? Notice changes in your feelings and enquire within as to their meaning. Question if your thoughts are based on reality or built up in your ego. It takes patience and persistence, but calm waters are waiting.

It is easy to become lost at times on the journey to self-discovery, overthinking and strongly identifying with our stories. If you notice yourself observing life instead of participating, take stock. Look to the checklist in chapter seven, 'Lift your mood' and the Mindfulness section, as an aid to ground yourself. Then, return your focus to this moment to restore energy balance and live fully in the flow of life.

Be in the flow:

- When in the flow of life, we become lost in our experience, fully participating with pure, positive, creative energy.

- Swimming against the tide of life is exhausting physically and mentally.

- Our thoughts are personal preferences that exist to help us navigate the world. In recognising these thoughts are not always in line with reality, we open the door to move back into presence.

- Working with our feelings is the way to happiness and success.

   ◦ Positive = in the flow of life.

   ◦ Negative = time to change energy to action or to change our thinking.

- If it isn't possible to change something causing our negative emotions, we can convert our energy of resistance to positive action.

- If you can't help yourself, be the source for someone else. Give because you want to, not expecting anything in return.

Q When would you say you feel most in the flow of life?

Dance along

When life doesn't go to plan,

When unhappy with our lot,

We are living in thought.

Life plays out its merry dance.

Stay rooted in frustration or fury, shouting,

"It shouldn't be like this!"

Life isn't happening to us.

Life happens.

It is for us to

Learn to dance along.

Go with the flow of life

Rediscover The Creator Within

twelve

Gratitude

Gratitude is grounding.
It sets the scene for future creation.

Gratitude comes from the Latin word gratus, meaning pleasing, acceptable, agreeable, thankful, and welcome. It is the quality of being thankful and appreciative of that which is meaningful to you.

Our nature is to want more. We create surplus food supplies, collect more possessions, strive for a bigger house, a higher-spec car, and more holidays when possible. We are, after all, co-creators of the world we inhabit, hungry for new experiences. Perhaps whilst striving for more, we could also appreciate what life has already provided, to be happier with what is?

How we think affects our perception of our world and sets our trajectory. Put another way, the world we see reflects our state of mind, our imagination. When you notice a common daisy, what do you see? A weed? A common flower? A memory, or perhaps an intricate thing of tremendous perfection and beauty?

There are many studies into gratitude and how it can boost self-esteem, happiness, bonding, improve sleep, increase immunity and longevity and decrease depression and anxiety. Practising gratitude helps to hone our positive imagination, to develop a more satisfying personal world. Is it perhaps worth our attention?

Before you read beyond this chapter, I challenge you to stop and appreciate the things you have around you; pets, people, nature, gifts of character, all past or present, that fill you with good emotion. These feelings are the secret to forming the world you see around you and will increase your enjoyment of life.

One moment of gratitude is excellent; creating a regular practice is even better. Regularly writing down what you are grateful for and the emotions these experiences arouse will provide more profound and longer-lived positive effects.

The rewarding consequences may not be immediately apparent. However, with persistence and patience, the benefits of your practice will become evident as you shift your focus away from negative thoughts.

When would be the best time during your day to think or scribble a few lines of appreciation? How many days will you commit to recording gratitude? Thinking of and taking time to move into the feeling of something you are grateful for as you wake, e.g. the sound of bird song, can help set your mood for the day.

Another helpful exercise is to notice what it is in these experiences that kindles gratitude in you. Understanding why you have these feelings can be a compass to your core values and what you want more in your life.

For example:

- All my life, I wanted to be a mother of two girls. When I look at my growing girls now, my heart wells with love and gratitude that my wish has come true. What is it about this experience that makes me feel gratitude when I recall the details? The fact that I had a dream and created it in my world. I love my children entirely and **learn and grow with them.**

- My dog Barney is a daft brown cockapoo and is always excited to explore or lie by my feet. As I stroke his ears or rub his tummy, he wriggles excitedly on his back. Watching him fills me with love and gratitude for his fluffy, loving little being. What is it about this experience that makes me feel gratitude? Barney's unconditional love, the loving connection we have and recognising that being **together is joyful.**

- My friends fill me with such delight. It is so easy for me to be grateful for each one of them. **Togetherness with them is joyful. I grow and learn** when I am with them, sharing in the highs and lows of life in **acceptance** that we are all imperfectly perfect.

As time progresses, it will be necessary to be more specific to 'wire your brain' for positive habits. For example, "I am grateful for my girls" is significant. To delve profoundly is to appreciate fully. "I am grateful for the quick wit of my youngest daughter who had us in stitches at the dinner table this evening. With the laughter she brought us, I felt closer and happier with my brood".

When we identify why we feel gratitude, our compass points towards our core values (mine are bold). When we honour our core values, we find ourselves in the flow of life.

Therefore, you can also determine your core values if you think of a time you felt in energetic flow when you felt on top of the world. What was it about this time that made you feel that way? The values you will identify are aspects of life that you appreciate. Core values are incredibly varied and unique to each person. They will become clear as we work through the exercises in the following pages. In committing your thoughts to paper, patterns will be easier to spot. Asking a trusted friend to write down your list can help your ideas to flow.

Writing out notes for what brings us joy and pleasure provides direction for a future that will deliver the most incredible opportunity for contentment.

Exercise: Gratitude

The top things I am grateful for and why

What am I grateful for?

_____

_____

_____

_____

What is it about this experience that elicits gratitude?

_____

_____

_____

My top core values are:

_____

_____

_____

_____

_____

_____

Exercise: Core values

An experience in which I felt in the flow of life

What was the experience? (Think of a time you felt on top of the world.) How did I feel?

_____

_____

_____

The top core values I identify with are:

_____

_____

_____

You may be questioning why we have moved to past examples when the overriding message is to guide you to presence; to this moment. As we start practising gratitude, we often automatically begin with past events. Our aim is to become familiar with the feeling of gratitude, and in doing so, learn to appreciate more in our lives, in this moment.

The default setting for most of us has likely been a strong identification with our past and future, not recognising that our essence lies beyond our imagined stories. Here we transition from identification with thought to choosing and directing our thinking. By focusing on positives from our past, we determine what experiences we would like more of in the future.

With practice and becoming accomplished at creating a healthy environment around us, we feel more and more in life's flow. When in the flow, we are in our positive, empowering state of creation, bringing harmony to ourselves and those around us.

Our nature, in presence, is a beautiful, blissful place to be, a place of creation—the creation of the experiences we wish to sample in life.

When we practice gratitude, there is noticeably more to appreciate in the present, bringing a clear focus to all the gifts around us. All things can be 'added' to you when you start at a place of acceptance and gratitude for what is.

"Gratitude turns what we have into enough"—Anonymous:

- Our nature is continuous change. We will never reach our destination of complete contentment with our lot because we are creators, always moving on to the next experience.
- We can, however, stop and smell the flowers we have planted and nurture them en route.
- How we think affects how we perceive our world and sets our trajectory.
- Practising gratitude boosts self-esteem, happiness, and bonding; it improves sleep, increases immunity and longevity, and decreases depression and anxiety.
- One moment of gratitude is excellent; creating a regular practice enables us to recognise more beauty and joy in real-time.

- Practising gratitude helps to hone our skills in positive imagination. By being specific about why we feel gratitude, our brains become 'wired' to the positive.
- By identifying why we feel gratitude, our compass points towards our core values. These values, when honoured, allow us to feel good, uplifted, alive, and in the flow of life.
- Gratitude is an entry point to presence.

Rediscover The Creator Within

thirteen

The labels we give ourselves

In a world without comparison,

who would you be?

If all people were 6'3", who would be tall? If everyone weighed 200 lbs, who would be fat or thin? What is tall without short, hard without easy, silence without noise, past without future, good without evil? Is it opposites or the attention to differences that generates something from nothing in human experience? If a tree falls in a forest and there is no one to hear it, does it make a sound? Does it matter until there is consciousness to think about it?

We use comparison to make sense of the world in which we live. Differences and similarities become labels and build a framework for identification and reference. In doing so, we engineer a self-conjured projection of who we believe ourselves and others to be.

Once the labels are in place, we rarely recognise them and take them on as a fact of reality. For example: "Delighted to meet you. I am Charles, eldest of three brothers, husband to Aisla and father to two children. I am a Lawyer, and in my spare time, I am passionate about golf and love to ski in Europe for our annual holiday."

Charles has a substantial picture in his head about who he believes he is, adding a feeling of security to his unique place in the world. As we read, we may compare ourselves to Charles to build a mental picture of his life and reaffirm the image we have of our own, all in imagination. Is Charles perhaps pompous, aloof, clever, wealthy, lucky? What other labels would you add, and who does this make him in comparison to you?

This comparison makes us feel more or less than the other person. Even in complaining about other people, typically noting a shortcoming, we endeavour to feel 'more than' or 'less than' another and add positively or negatively to our energy. What and who we believe ourselves to be, we 'become'. Who we believe others to be, they become in our eyes.

**Comparison with others is peaceful
when made in loving acceptance of what is.**

If fate took the labels Charles has adopted one by one, his wife leaves, the firm announces his redundancy, and his children refuse to see him, would he be any less? So he may feel it, yet his intrinsic nature lies beyond his labels and away from those given by others. Why then is it so hard for us to accept ourselves as 'enough'?

Catching and quieting our discriminations over differences can enable us to stop spiralling thought patterns and return to our nature of innate peace, well-being, and neutral balance without judgment of ourselves or others.

The less loving and accepting we are of ourselves, the less loving and accepting we become of others. Perhaps we have lessons to learn from nature. Imagine the penguin berating itself because it can't fly, the vulture eating in secret, ashamed as it feeds on carrion when other birds eat berries or the golden eagle embarrassed by its size whilst wistfully watching the hummingbird dart from flower to flower. Do they question their place in creation, or do they follow their instincts? Is it not clear to see each is perfectly created for the space it occupies in the Universe?

At our core, all are equal. Nothing can be added or taken away, only thoughts about who we perceive ourselves to be. Challenging thinking about ourselves and others (without judging the thoughts we have about our thoughts) is a way to return to a peaceful mind.

We all talk to ourselves, internally or externally and perpetually 'sit' in judgment based on the scripts we have penned so far in life. Then, of course, genetics play their part, providing us with a tendency towards certain traits. However, even these genetic traits are impermanent and change in subtle shifts, moulded by our life experience. So, for example, an introvert may decide that they enjoy being the centre of attention on occasion.

Hence, we become who we think we are. We refine our should and should not's, becoming more rigid in our thinking as we age. Nevertheless, the labels we attribute are influential and always 'right' to our mind if given often enough or felt deeply.

I am gregarious.	I am not fun to be with.
I am shy.	I am outgoing.
I am ugly.	I am beautiful.
I am hardworking.	I am lazy.
I am not intelligent.	I am knowledgeable.
I am fat.	I am skinny.
I am wealthy.	I am poor.
I am confident.	I am not good at much.
I am unlovable.	I AM LOVE.

Each of these labels is conjured internally and could be seen or argued to be untrue. Love is innate, and therefore, 'I am love' is the only natural label. If this raises questions for you, I invite you to meditate on this or keep the idea in mind to draw your conclusions over the next few days.

If someone tells us we are different from our adopted labels, it can cause hurt, confusion, insecurity, or even fury. The illusion, and at the same time, the truth, if only at surface level, is that we are who we think ourselves to be. I am as I think and feel, or stripping it back to a clean slate, I AM.

No thought is an enemy. We need only harness it. We have a solid foundation for building the life we wish to live by questioning the validity of unuseful thinking and embracing positive, constructive ideas about ourselves.

As an example, let us take the situation of a messy divorce. Months of court battles and bitter rows leave the two parties exhausted. How are they to move forward to new happy lives? Unfortunately, their acrimonious state of sadness, bitterness and anger is often the path, leaving the predetermined world of their egos to play out. Negative emotions are the easy route when everyone is exhausted, yet these feelings call for action to change circumstances or thinking.

Catching the stories their minds tell, 'I am not lovable', 'I will never find love again', 'I am not worthy of love', 'I can't trust my judgement', 'I am impossible to live with', and questioning whether these statements are factual, is vital. Well-directed thinking can conjure a new empowering script for positive emotion and character. We can redirect energy by writing down and obliterating one poor thought at a time and replacing them with a positive:

- I choose self-love.
- I am lovable.

- Love will find me when I am ready.
- I am enough.
- I add to the joy in someone else's life, and they mirror this back to me.

Noticing what is real in the present and changing their perspective, the couple can choose to let go of all gathered thoughts about their failed marriage, their ex and themselves, and move to a brighter future.

We are creators of all thought and feeling, shaping our existence. Negative thinking is so much easier than positive—in the short term. Watching thoughts, feelings and emotions with awareness is one of the keys to being in the flow of life and realising our dreams.

Who do you believe you are? A powerful exercise is to notice the labels you have placed on yourself as you 'hear' them. Think deeply; question if they are real because you have a fresh start available to you. Many successful people around you have chosen to silence numerous limiting thoughts and hone their positive ones. Time to train your thinking to serve you? Write down a new empowering 'label' in the present tense and pin it somewhere you will see it often.

Our inner world is reflected by what we talk about, e.g. I'll never find the perfect partner; I am a rubbish parent; I am not a valued employee; I am a terrible friend; I am not good at anything. When a story of woe is on repeat, perhaps it is the time to face reality, put pen to paper and create your perfect mind.

When we learn to control our inner conversation, we see the results in our external world. Labels are, in reality, transitional expressions of thought. Will you choose going forward to respect yourself in awareness and harness an empowering point of view?

Exercise:

Thoughts from a new perspective

At this juncture, we are considering the negative thoughts we hold about ourselves. So, first, write out a negative thought (please work on one at a time)

Thought:

_____

_____

_____

Question the truth objectively as if you were your own best friend—work with a friend if it helps. Reverse your negative statement, so for example, 'I am not good enough' becomes 'I AM good enough.' Give supporting evidence using decisive, reinforcing language as to why the positive is true.

Truth. Give evidence if appropriate:

_____

_____

_____

_____

_____

_____

_____

If you find yourself unable to cross out your original statement, what new thought has arisen from your exercise? Write down this new self-deprecating thought and restart. For example, 'I am not good enough' may become 'I am not good enough at...' or an entirely new negative for you to challenge.

Finally, when you feel the truth of your new affirmation, cross out your original negative.

I AM

_____

_____

_____

_____

_____

In evolving in this practice, we catch thoughts that are not constructive and tackle them one at a time before they become feelings, to step into the life of which we dream. Negative thinking is here to serve, to be noticed, questioned and used to affect positive change. Change your thoughts, change your life; then, negativity wipes away in a moment of awareness, creating space for an exciting new chapter.

Positive labels are empowering as long as we recognise we are taking ownership of something borrowed. If we think of the small child, who becomes inconsolable when a toy is taken away from them: "Mine, mine!" sound the insistent cries. Many of us continue in this vein throughout our whole lives. A job is lost, and it feels personal. A relationship ends, and we feel broken. A limb amputated in an accident, and life feels unbearable. Age takes our beauty, we feel invisible, wealth diminishes, and we are like the small child crying for what is lost. All is temporary, on loan, and when 'taken away', we are no less, despite thoughts that arise to the contrary. Time brings change, yet we remain whole. Only our thoughts tell us life should be different from reality.

There is a space clear of thought, free from all theoretical ideas of who we are when in presence. When we let go of the roles we play, mother, father, husband, wife, daughter, son, parent, employee, all our learning, all life experience, what lies beneath is a clean slate. When we notice the awareness behind our thoughts, nothing vanishes. All that is 'us', beyond our ego programs, is waiting to resume as before–if that is our wish.

I Am

At this moment,

I release all expectations

of what should and should not be.

I let go of everything I know.

I let go of all ideas about who I am,

all thought of the roles I live.

Gone is the persona of a partner,

parent, child, student, worker.

I let go of all learning, knowledge and life experience.

What is left?

Now, in this moment, who am I?

In clear thought, our needless grasping at life in an attempt to hang onto everything that, by nature, is impermanent diminishes. Our need for labels wanes, and the possessiveness of our ego becomes soothed.

The words we think and speak gain power and become our reality. In present awareness, only empowering thoughts enter the mind whilst accepting the impermanence of all things.

The space taken by 'I am not enough' and 'I am enough', 'everything is going against me' and 'all is as it should be' is the difference between being lost in the fog of life and being in the blissful state of presence.

Every one of us at some time believes we should be more. So few accept ourselves as enough. In gratitude for your attributes, how are you 'enough'?

Exercise:

The top things I like about myself

What attribute or gift am I grateful for?

_____

_____

_____

What is it about this that elicits gratitude?

_____

_____

_____

_____

Do your labels empower you and those around you?

- We use comparison to make sense of the world in which we live. Differences and similarities become labels and build a framework for identification and reference.

- Once the labels are in place, we rarely recognise them and take them on as a fact of reality.

- What and who we believe ourselves to be, we 'become'. Who we believe others to be, they become in our eyes.

- Catching and quieting our discriminations over differences is a step in returning to our nature of innate peace, well-being, and neutral balance without judgment of ourselves or others.

- The less loving and accepting we are of ourselves, the less loving and accepting we become of others.

- Wherever we are on our journey in life, we are 'enough'.

- Nothing can be added or taken away, only thoughts about who we perceive ourselves to be.

- Negative thinking is here to serve, to be noticed, questioned and used to affect positive change.

- Slay one negative thought at a time. Write down a new empowering 'label' in the present tense and pin it somewhere you will see it often.
- Watching thoughts, feelings and emotions with awareness is one of the keys to being in the flow of life and realising our dreams.
- When we learn to control our inner conversation, we see the results in our external world.

Q What is innate in all of us that cannot be taken away?

Q "Comparison with others is peaceful when made in loving acceptance of what is." What does this mean?

Rediscover The Creator Within

fourteen

From judgement
to loving acceptance

Only our thoughts lead us to
happiness or unhappiness.

A t our core, we are all alike, yet cultural, societal,
familial, and educational experiences are different.
The people we interact with give us a life experience and
perception of reality that may vary wildly, even to another
person down the same street.

The result? We 'wear' all our worldly experiences and
expectations of life borne on the path WE have trodden.
Because we experience life a certain way, does that mean
we live the ultimate reality? We perceive a truth of
existence based on our human boundaries, limitations
and understanding. What could a fish know about
running on Africa's planes or a cheetah about becoming

an astronaut? What could a human understand beyond human limitations? What can an individual truly know about the experience of others beyond their personal reality? Each living creature has a unique viewpoint, the only perspective they can completely grasp. So what is reality?

Every one of us acts and behaves within the boundaries of our worldliness. Every life is a distinctive experience with differing expectations. As the 1895 Mary T. Lathrap poem suggests, "Walk a mile in his moccasins" before acting other than in compassion, kindness, empathy, and understanding.

In fully comprehending that we paint the canvas of our reality based on the labels we place on people and things, we see how we create our mood and life experience. It is natural to put tags on roles such as partner, mother, child, authority figures etc. That is how we define things outside of our human form and set expectations of future interactions. With a calm and present mind, is it reasonable to state that when 'others' fail to reach our expectations, our thinking must change rather than becoming inflamed at the 'inefficiencies' of the other?

When we see reality as our own and believe that others should conform to our perspective of life, WE cause our unrest and disharmony. Who are you blaming for your unhappiness? Hopefully, the power of your thought is becoming evident. Of course, other people can set emotion on a path, yet you have ultimate control. Only one person is genuinely in charge of your happiness and goals, and that person is you.

Parents are a common 'source of suffering'. Mother or Father, the 'voice' associated with the criticisms played in our adult mind that we place on ourselves in reality. Parents are souls who came to earth a moment before us. Perhaps they were/are still on auto-pilot, running one feeling into the next without thought of effect in action or word.

As a grown adult, no person has the power to make you feel positive or negative for more than a moment—when you are present and consciously aware of your emotions. The person they were last time you met can, if you choose, be different next time you are together. On one visit, you can feel them selfish and negative; on the next, loving and caring. It is all a matter of thought. You hold all the power to decide if you will allow negative emotion, neutrality, joy or pain.

Partners would also be high on the list for those who 'make our lives difficult'. Many of us get annoyed with our partners for something they do or fail to do. When their behaviour falls short of our expectations, we naively believe they should be other than they are, different from their ego program built over a lifetime.

Is this thinking not absurd? When we see reality as our own and believe that others should conform to our perspective of life, WE cause our unrest and disharmony. In presence, we see others are just living life; they do not make us angry, happy or sad; they do not have that power. We, however, do have the ability to make ourselves feel other than at peace. In blaming others for our unhappiness, we add labels to who 'they are' rather than accept our journey is to act in love, adding harmony to the world. Remember, negative emotions are not wrong or bad, as feelings and emotions are a compass to our happiness.

Becoming aware of the thought patterns that render us less than loving to another soul can be challenging. It is hard knowing it is all down to you, and you can no longer blame someone else! But, when we start to change our ego programs and notice our thoughts, old behaviour patterns often persist. This slavery to past action is followed closely by recognising our folly once again, in present awareness.

Presence offers the gift of forgiveness of others and ourselves. Knowing each of us is uniquely responsible for our thoughts and feelings, we have a strong foundation for a life of love. Every day will offer small victories as we become enlightened to our thinking.

Daily life with others is challenging when run at such a fast pace. It takes work to remain in calm awareness, especially with our most prominent teachers, the people closest to us. The people who leave the toilet seat up or load the dishwasher 'incorrectly'. The children we need to tell ten times to tidy their room. The colleagues who make our blood boil. Without a calm and present mind, it would be easy to blame them for our frustrations and unhappiness.

Only thoughts lead us to be happy or unhappy. When we live in presence with self-love, negative labels fall away one at a time, from ourselves and others.

Every one of us is imperfectly perfect

In presence, we understand there is only one person responsible for our despair and unhappiness, ourselves. Life is not happening to us. Life unfolds, and we decide how to feel about it. Sorrow, joy, hate, fear, and all other emotions are added only by our thinking. We can use what life presents, with self-love, to our benefit.

In presence, there is no retrospective judgement for our past. There is no judgment for times lost in thought patterns about who others should have been or how life should have differed. There is no judgement for times we were less than loving. Instead, we can assess why emotions are out of sync, learn and move forwards with a new awareness.

When we speak from a place of presence, all words that arise come from love, leading to harmony; our thought patterns become easier to spot, helping traverse a world that would have previously entrapped us in conflict. Compromise is made willingly in love, knowing there is no right or wrong, only how we think.

We are of love, and all action that moves us toward love creates harmony.

Love is all

I come to life in love.

I leave in love.

What else is there?

All else I add unto me.

All else I add unto you.

Living in harmony and acceptance:

- Only our thoughts lead us to happiness or unhappiness.
- What can we truly know about the experience of others when it falls beyond our personal experience?
- Every one of us acts and behaves within the boundaries of our experience.
- When others 'fail' to reach our expectations, the most efficient and peaceful response available to us is to challenge our thinking.
- Only one person is genuinely in charge of your happiness and goals, and that person is you. As a grown adult, no person has the power to make you feel a certain way for more than a moment.
- Having negative emotions is not wrong or bad. Emotions are a compass to your bliss. Trust your intuition to know when to change your thinking or your situation.
- Presence offers the gift of forgiveness of others and yourself.

- Knowing you are uniquely responsible for your thoughts and feelings, you have a firm foundation for a life lived in love.
- It takes work to remain calm, especially with our most prominent teachers, the people closest to us.
- In presence, compromise is made willingly in love, knowing there is no right or wrong, only how we think.

Rediscover The Creator Within

fifteen

Life is a mirror

Our persistent words of complaint show a
true reflection for all who look to see.

A s you become efficient at labelling your emotions,
initially, it is easy to point the finger of blame at
others for causing your unrest. However, as you evolve in
the upcoming practice, negative emotions disperse before
finger-pointing begins.

When we complain about a person regularly, our
words carry a surprising message that, when examined,
lead to the only behaviour we can 100% affect.

- We cannot change other people.
- We cannot change the past.
- Events could not have unfolded differently.
- Thinking otherwise is a wish.
- Thinking otherwise is self-induced suffering.

Blame and anger are toxic,
harming ourselves and those around us.

Practising the Mirror Technique diffuses the emotional burden of past events, making space for a peaceful life. When we work with The Mirror Technique for everyday scenarios, our minds become more present by dispelling drama before it has time to build.

When you notice yourself complaining for the umpteenth time, hold up your virtual mirror to see if the label you attribute to the defendant is watertight 100% of the time. Then, look to see how your complaint applies to you.

Our intention is not to shift the direction of blame but to dissolve the feelings causing the depreciation in your relationship. Bear in mind some of us use sweeping generalisations when we are unhappy. Turn your statement around in every possible way to 'feel' different perspectives. Not all will be right but take your time, and you will know when you hit the nail on the head. Change comes with a willingness to see things differently. For example:

"He doesn't listen to me" (He never listens to you EVER?) becomes:

He does listen to me, or even, I don't listen to him.

"She doesn't understand how hard I work" (EVER?) becomes:

I don't understand how hard she works or, she does understand how hard I work.

"He doesn't compliment me on my appearance" to:

He does compliment me on my appearance or, I don't compliment him on his appearance or, I don't compliment myself on my appearance.

"They never recognise my achievements" to:

They do recognise my achievements or, I don't recognise their achievements or, I don't recognise my achievements.

You can complete these exercises in your head, but seeing reality in black and white is more compelling. It can help prevent becoming re-embroiled in old stories, adding another layer of detachment. Working on a screen is OK if you will not be distracted.

Exercise:

The Mirror Technique–Complaints

Before you begin your exercise:

1. Take a few deep breaths to centre yourself and come to a calm presence.
2. Open your mind.

What is my complaint?

_____

_____

_____

_____

_____

_____

What are the mirrored perspectives?

You can use The Mirror Technique for all persistent thoughts, minor niggles or significant haunting memories. Trauma distorts our current reality making life feel more daunting. For memories of trauma, abuse and physical harm, it can take a great deal of presence to see your way to accepting the resolutions without guidance. Trust yourself to know when you are ready to face difficult memories and ask for help if you need it.

Honour yourself by taking time to answer this exercise from your heart. Be the witness to your thoughts as if you are watching a movie or helping a friend. Completing this following exercise with a friend can help keep you focused on the questions without losing yourself in your story. When your thoughts wander, inducing unhelpful feelings in real-time, bring yourself back to this moment with a deep breath. Use your positive memory anchor if necessary.

Looking at what we believe 'should' have happened, we highlight where we are apportioning blame. This blame and desire to rewrite history is the cause of our hurt in real-time. We cannot change the past, but we do have now, this moment, to self soothe with emotional intelligence.

Before you complete your self-exploration exercise and get the most out of this process, take a minute or two to bring yourself to this moment with a few deep breaths. A mindfulness exercise will further aid in calming your mind and 'ground' you in reality.

Now, are you OK? We are all OK for the vast majority of our lives—only thinking back to challenging events makes us feel out of balance. In recalling a challenging event, we may not 'feel' OK. Still, in truth, we have everything we need to return ourselves to a calm state and dispel negative thinking, the root of our unrest.

If we continue in the same patterns we always have, we obtain the same results. Change takes the intentional direction of our energies.

Exercise: The Mirror Technique

Example 1

What is the specific memory that is causing negative emotion?

Following a falling out with my parents, which led to years of animosity between us, we tried to patch things up. However, as I left their house, my Dad said, "It would have been easier if you had died."

How I reacted: I understood what he meant, but the comment cut deep into me, and I felt great pain and rejection all over again. "He wishes I had died to save his hurt?" At that point, my pain was too great to make any more effort at reconciliation.

What 'should' have happened: He should have loved me more.

He should have never left me at my lowest point in life.

He should have made more of an effort at reconciliation.

What is causing your distress now, at this moment?

My thoughts bring back negative physical feelings of hurt and despair–how I felt at the time. I have added more negative experiences with my parents since that date, cutting deeper.

Am I OK?

Yes, I Am OK (but I still feel rubbish)

Hold up your imaginary mirror to see events from a different point of view.

"He should have loved me more." He meant;

It would not have been easier if you had died and I hurt because I miss you, or it would have been so hard if you had died because I could never have told you how much I love you.

"He should have never left me at my lowest." He should have left me at my lowest because it made me the emotionally strong woman I am today.

"He should have made more of an effort at reconciliation." His pain was so great I should have made more of an effort at reconciliation. But, unfortunately, neither my parents nor I had the emotional intelligence to understand we each had to make more effort to patch up our relationship.

When you can 'feel' your lesson, look over your exercise and see if your ego is still trying to hang onto what is right and wrong. Your response may be a desperate bid to keep your familiar story to justify your emotion and behaviour.

If life experiences had led people to a different action, they would have behaved differently, yourself included. The mirror technique highlights alternative points of view by looking at the situation from all available angles, dispelling the heavy finger of blame that causes our pain. It is imperative that we also let go of any blame we could attribute to ourselves. It is as it is. The past is gone, the future not yet real.

No judgement is necessary.

Nothing is personal

until we make it so in our thoughts.

Example 2

What is the specific memory that is causing negative emotion?

We were having a chocolate egg hunt for our girls and their cousins. Alan, my husband, was impatient with the girls and grumbled at them to find their eggs. He always ruins the moment when we should be making memories for our girls!

How I reacted: I was very cross and left the garden in a huff.

What should he have done: He should have had more fun with the girls and help create happy memories. He should not have been grumpy and impatient.

What is causing your distress now, at this moment?

Thinking about his behaviour makes me feel cross and sad for the girls.

Now, at this moment, am I OK?

Yes, but thinking about it makes me unhappy. I need to change my thinking.

History unfolds, made of every moment that precedes it. People behave according to the information available to them and their level of awareness in a particular moment. What 'should' have happened is YOUR wish, not reality.

Hold up your imaginary mirror to see events from a different point of view.

He should have been grumpy and impatient. He had bought the eggs our girls had requested. When we knew my sister was coming to visit, he went out of his way to buy more eggs. The ones he had for our girls were out of stock, so he got different eggs for my nephew and niece. I put the eggs out in the garden. He wanted the girls to have the ones he had bought for them. He spent time choosing eggs to hide. He IS fun, caring and considerate and does work to create happy memories for our girls.

I should not be grumpy and impatient. I left the garden in a mood before the children finished the chocolate hunt. I was the one who could ruin the girl's memories.

It is normal to look for someone or something to blame for our issues. As our emotional intelligence evolves, we come to see the holes in our finger-pointing stories of blame. We can turn disapproval onto ourselves in the often startling realisation that we alone are responsible for our emotions. Be gentle, be kind with yourself. If your experiences up to that point were different, you would have acted differently. No judgement is necessary. Nothing is personal, just life unfolding.

Exercise:

The Mirror Technique–Reflection

What is the specific memory that is causing negative emotion?

Bring your thoughts to a moment in time that causes you suffering and recall the details. How did you react? What do you believe 'should' have happened?:

_____

_____

_____

_____

_____

_____

What is causing your distress now, at this moment?

Clue–only your thoughts can cause your suffering when recalling the past.

Now, at this moment, am I OK?

Breathe deeply, put your hand on your heart to bring yourself to this moment.

The answer is NO; I am in danger and must change my situation. Or YES; I have enough to sustain my life and must change my thinking to return my mind to calm.

History unfolds, made of every moment that precedes it. People behave according to the information available to them and their level of awareness in a particular moment. What 'should' have happened is YOUR wish, not reality.

Hold up your imaginary mirror to see events from a different point of view.

Your perspective causes all emotion. It is natural to hold onto stories to justify long-held beliefs and behaviours. Reverse the 'should have' statements to see alternative views.

_____

_____

_____

_____

_____

_____

_____

First, take the plank from your eye:

- If you are not yet ready to face your past, use your positive memories as an anchor to bring back a good feeling.
- Only your thinking about the past causes your emotions to change.
- Blame and anger are toxic, harming ourselves and those around us.
  - We cannot change other people.
  - We cannot change the past.
  - Events could not have unfolded differently.
  - Thinking otherwise is a wish.
  - Thinking otherwise is self-induced suffering.
- By looking at what we believe 'should' have happened, we highlight where we apportion blame.
- Looking at a situation from another perspective can dispel building unrest in relationships. It takes a desire for harmony and stillness in presence to truly see another's point of view when emotions are high.

- Use the Mirror Technique whenever you feel emotions changing negatively with another person. With practice, you will shorten the time you spend in discord.
- The Mirror Technique
  - What is the situation that is causing me distress?
  - What is causing distress at this moment?
  - In reality, am I OK now, at this moment?
  - What is a different perspective? Try out a 180° reversal.

Life is a mirror

Rediscover The Creator Within

sixteen

Free will

We can consciously direct life at our will
when we are aware of our thoughts and feelings
in the present moment.

Our biology and experience predetermine our lives. Each action determines the next until we step into free will. Free Will is available to us when we become present. There is no right or wrong in presence, no judgment, in the awareness that all is as it should be.

**Free Will is the ability to choose "otherwise,"
in a predetermined life run in the subconscious.
When we emerge in the conscious,
present world, we direct our fate
within the parameters of unfolding creation.**

We could argue that, for example, imprisonment or debilitating illness infringe our free will. That assumption would be incorrect. Our freedom to be as we wish may alter, yet we have the privilege to decide how we respond to the circumstances in which we find ourselves. Free will is the mind's activity coming from present awareness in accepting what is, regardless of our circumstances.

A child lands hands down in a muddy puddle. Do they cry and lament their sorry wet, dirty situation, or squeal with delight and jump up and down, encouraging others to join in?

In acceptance of our present, we choose how to feel and direct our future at will.

Predetermined action or free will?

Experience

Free Will
(Choice made in your aware,
meditative presence.
A step rarely taken.)

Emotion
(Feelings are added running in
the auto-pilot of the
subconscious.)

Thought or
Spontaneous Feeling
(A physical response
produced in the body.)

Ego Thought
(Thoughts added based
on all experience.)

The outside wheel of the diagram shows our auto-pilot mode, where the subconscious predetermines life. One action leads to the next with very little conscious thought.

For example:

Experience—A loved one speaks harshly to you.

Thought or Spontaneous Feeling—You have a thought, for example, what did I do wrong, that isn't very nice, what is wrong with them, etc., or you react spontaneously for protection.

Ego thought—Your subconscious programs search your data banks for past related events and guide how the situation is likely to play out, providing automatic responses.

Emotion—The body joins in by pumping hormones based on your current circumstances AND the memories you are revisiting, fueling your feelings and emotions. You then add this growing emotional state to your next similar experience when your subconscious triggers these feelings and memories once again.

You can step out of the predetermined world of the subconscious auto-pilot at any stage on the map by moving into presence and questioning what is true at this moment. All questions are asked and answered in the first person, bearing in mind that you can only change only one person in this world. You always have Free Will to choose how you feel.

Experience—Original experience, e.g. a loved one speaks harshly.

Thought or reaction—Q Is my thought accurate and appropriate at this moment?

Do I need to change my situation or change my perspective?

Ego Thought—Q Am I adding fuel to this situation?

Is my thought accurate and appropriate at this moment?

Do I need to change my situation or change my perspective?

Emotion—Q Is this emotion proportionate to this circumstance in this moment?

Do I need to change my situation or change my perspective?

Everything that happens in the world is a physical reality (maybe). How we feel about our experience is our choice and shapes our truth to the positive or negative. Experience, commented upon within our minds, creates the opposites of good and evil; we choose how we think about our experience within the constraints of our limited human perspective.

When we step into presence, we see reality as it is. We drop our stories, knowing life as an impersonal unfolding to experience as we choose.

Free Will in presence:

- Free Will is available to us when we become present.

- We can decide how we respond to the circumstances in which we find ourselves. So often, we react on auto-pilot without conscious thought. A life lived in the subconscious is predetermined by our past.

- Free will is the mind's activity coming from present awareness in accepting what is, regardless of our circumstances.

- In acceptance of our present, we choose how to feel and direct our future at will.

Q If I ask, "if there is an omnipotent, loving presence, why does it allow suffering?" Can you now answer this question?

Life perfectly orchestrated

Life is perfectly orchestrated.
13.8 billion years of creation,
Delivering this moment here, now,
the entirety of life in an absolute balanced order.

In awareness, I am witness
to the eternal flow of alpha and omega.
Nothing to something,
Something to nothing.

Creation is my form,
impermanence in my design.
Energy infinitely changing,
Balance perpetually restored.

Free will

seventeen

Self-love

Loving acceptance of ourselves,

knowing that we are all 'enough',

is key to a harmonious, loving world.

Good relationships keep us happier and healthier, and all relationships start with the one with ourselves. Self-love is not selfish but graceful. In practising self-love, we are kind and gentle to ourselves, and the by-product is that we are kind and gentle to others.

When we turn the magnifying glass onto ourselves and feel unhappy about any aspect or attribute, our behaviour likely changes to the negative, and we withdraw or act out! How we think about ourselves affects those around us. By being kind to ourselves, stress diminishes as destructive thoughts and actions dissipate, returning us and the world around to harmony.

It all starts with you. Your energy feeds out and back in again, often at a similar level and tone to whence it left. How could we know we are love unless we have been less than loving to another or ourselves? Being less than loving hurts us. Change or movement away from our intrinsic calm, loving nature, we feel at our heart. In stillness, we 'just are' with nothing to experience.

Changes in our feelings create a shift of energy away from our innate harmonious nature, like ripples on a still ocean. WE set these ripples or waves of energy in motion, exploring our existence, firstly regarding others and then ourselves. Interaction with others and exploring our experiences allows us to become self-aware, recognising how our feelings, words, and actions affect our world. The more self-aware and self loving we become, the calmer our ocean.

We can choose which feelings we wish to observe and which we allow to reside within us. Some feelings will lift the world; others will add to the chaos. Self-love is the start of unity and cohesion, and our individual and collective future is more certain when we learn to work together.

Have you noticed how, when someone shows an act of compassion, such as letting you pull out in traffic or offering to do something to lighten your load, or gifting something 'just because', you feel compelled to pass on the uplifting feeling it solicits? One act of kindness ripples out and affects many. Life feeds back the energy we give out.

Peace and harmony in presence are easy when there is just one person. But, as soon as there is someone to interact with, how do we know what is 'right' and good?

A 96-year-old mother lay in a coma in her final hours of life. Around her, the family were planning her funeral, being in acceptance of the inevitable. They live in a culture where burials take place, typically the day after death.

- One son wants to hold the funeral the day after his mother dies, already heavy with grief, having buried his dear wife less than a month previously.
- Two want to wait a day so that the grandchildren don't have to take a day off work as a holiday.

- A daughter in law hopes the funeral will be as soon as possible as she needs to get back to her recently widowed and grieving mother caring for her children.

Who comes first? If you don't honour yourself and express your wish, how can you be showing self-love? If you hurt another person, how can that be showing self-love? What of the judgements that arise in all concerned?

When emotions run high, it is easy for love to be clouded by a need to have some control. Is there one correct answer? We can only answer that in the space of presence that is 'now'. At the right time, the elderly mother, eternally brilliant and loving, made her own decision and gave her last breath when she was ready. That, of course, dictated when the funeral was. All feelings of aggravation towards who was right and how events 'should' unfold were all in our imagination. Decisions made in the 'right' moment offer honest guidance to the path of love.

We are all the sum of so many experiences, and it is impossible to do 'right' by everyone all the time whilst honouring our own needs. What is suitable for one person may feel hurtful to another, yet only thought, reflecting life experience, makes word and action appear right or wrong.

In reality, there is no right or wrong,
only kind thought and action in the moment.

We honour ourselves when we are in acceptance that we sometimes think differently to those around us, and that difference is OK. We work in love and kindness in present awareness, knowing that hurting others will lead to our pain. In accepting ourselves and understanding self-love, we see that WE cannot hurt anyone in our aim to be kind.

Despite our best efforts, people will sometimes be offended by our words and actions, but that is for them to deal with themselves. There is no way to please all people all of the time because we are all living such different experiences. However, we can be at peace knowing we have done what we can by being true to ourselves and, in doing so, acting in love.

Self-love

Love of self is kind, accepting, peaceful.
Love of self allows the love of others,
which is kind, accepting, and peaceful.

We are complete, each having a clean slate within, waiting to be directed in our true essence, that of love. When we understand this, we find the freedom in each moment to trust that life unfolds for us to embrace without fear or judgement.

Acting selfishly or spitefully against another person also causes our anguish by embroiling our minds and bodies in negative thoughts and feelings. We feel the pain we cause others. Self-love is the start point we move away from or towards in knowing we are enough. Life is a gift. Without self-care, life becomes painful and may be lost through injury or illness.

Be kind to yourself as you work through this chapter because you will likely turn the blame on yourself when the penny drops if any of the following applies to you. Life unfolds, and we act based on our level of consciousness at each moment. As there is only this moment, none of us could have acted any differently in the past.

The following may cause a reaction, so settle into a place of calm thoughtfulness for what follows. Remember, there is never any blame to attribute to yourself for where you find yourself today. Park the past.

After the initial abusive experience, in reality, as an adult, there is only one kind of abuse, self-abuse.

- You could not have acted differently.
- Be kind to yourself.
- Park the past.
- NOW is the key to your future.

Self-love in the context of abuse is a very emotional subject, and there are so many grey areas. The abused and abuser mirror low self-worth and perpetuate thinking patterns that damage themselves and those around them. It is for each individual to find their way to know they are worthy of love and happiness.

Self-abuse is when we believe negative thoughts about ourselves that we are not worthy of love or happiness. As adults, we are not living in self-love if we are abusive or remain in an abusive relationship.

Unpleasantness grows when innate love turns to selfishness through untrue self-given labels and thinking. The misguided desire leads us to attempt to feel 'more' by diminishing another. We can only add thoughts to ourselves or another, and ALL thought is a temporary illusion. If we inflict physical or mental pain on ourselves or others, we are not living in self-love. To harm another will hurt us. To harm ourselves will hurt others.

Physical abuse is never acceptable. Likewise, malicious, sustained verbal attacks are not OK. After the initial offensive experience, it can be incredibly challenging to see that we hold the key to our happiness when lost in fear, confusion or self-loathing. Nevertheless, there is always a choice as an adult, even though it may feel near impossible to make a change.

In cases of mental insult, hurtful words are believed and taken on as part of ourselves. These hurtful labels turn to self-abuse when we integrate them into our psyche. Feeling unworthy leads an individual to stay in a cycle of abuse, fear and hate, even though it is painful. Living with low self-esteem and feeling helplessly trapped, remaining with what we know invariably feels easier than moving into a world with so many unknowns. There is always help available if you need support.

Our historical choice to remain in the status quo (although not recognised as a choice whilst in the prison of the mind) is a form of self-punishment, not accepting our worth. You are enough. No judgement is ever necessary.

We can only be safe from mental or physical harm when we recognise our value and right to live free from pain and fear or when our survival instincts direct us to take action. In remembering we are worthy of self-love and self-respect, we are motivated to take the profoundly bold step to make a change–when the time is right.

In recognising we are worthy of self-love and self-respect, we are motivated to take deeply courageous steps to move to a blissful, fulfilling life.

N.B. Wouldn't it be wonderful to fix those around us? Alas, we can only change one person, and that person is ourselves. It is not for the victim to 'free' the abuser whilst in the grip of their captive mind. The abuser may find their way to understand that they are not the labels they have taken on as part of themselves, that they cannot make someone less to make themselves more, and do not practice self-love in hurting others. It is for every individual to find their way' home' to their true nature when ready.

This transition can never be forced and is something we move into when we are ready to recognise our worth. We may not have been taught love in childhood, yet each of us intuitively knows real love.

Who can we change? Is your way the only way? Are some of your relationships unloving, or are you adding an internal narrative that creates more animosity or emotional pain? Our intuition is crucial in knowing if we must change our circumstances or make a reasoned conscious choice to remain as we are and change our thoughts about our circumstances to create a harmonious world.

**The past does not define us and
to love and be loved is a gift waiting for all.**

Each of us is innately whole and perfect by nature. We must recognise that we are worthy of unconditional love and move into a life of harmony. Love begins with loving ourselves. When we rediscover a healthy love within us, we attract those who honour us and love wholeheartedly.

You may question 'rediscovering' a healthy love within ourselves. Love in presence is intrinsic. Love is who we all are, and this 'space' of presence is always available when we learn to quieten our minds. It is accessible when we become aware of our ego games and live consciously present. Nothing is taken away, and nothing is added to our nature that we do not allow in our thoughts. Every thought and action comes from within, never from others, despite the illusion. We choose which external experiences we filter out and which we integrate.

We alone define ourselves. We are all enough, and no person can add to or take away from our innate bliss and completeness.

Affirmation for self-love

I live knowing all are equal.

I direct all thought, word and deed in love.

I am accepting that

I can't please all the people all the time.

I forgive adverse reactions knowing that

I do my best in self-love and

the love I have for others.

I am enough:

- All relationships start with the one with ourselves.

- In practising self-love, we are kind and gentle to ourselves and others. There is no fight to be had.

- We are all the sum of so many experiences, and it is impossible to do 'right' by everyone all the time whilst honouring our own needs.

- Decisions made in the 'right' moment offer accurate guidance to the path of love.

- In reality, there is no right or wrong, only kind thought and action in the moment.

- When we come to complete acceptance and understanding of self-love, we see that we cannot hurt anyone else.

- When acting in love and kindness, people may still be offended by our actions.

- When we truly understand there is no way to please all the people all of the time, we find the freedom to trust that life unfolds for us to embrace without fear or judgement.

- Loving acceptance of yourself is key to a harmonious, loving world around you.

- Self-abuse is when we believe our negative thoughts and, or that someone else is causing our suffering.
- Every thought and action comes from within, never from outside us. There is nothing to be taken and nothing to be added, only thought about who we are.
- When we genuinely understand self-love, no person can add to or take away from our innate bliss and completeness.
- The past does not define us and to love and be loved is a gift waiting for us all.

Rediscover The Creator Within

eighteen

You are more powerful
than you know

Hopefully, by now, you have a good idea of how your thoughts become you. Dwelling on our worries reinforces negative thought patterns, inviting misfortune by creating a constant expectation of misery. It is easy to visualise and feel what we don't want. By allowing this habit, we get MORE of what we don't want. Listen to your thoughts and take the time to direct them to your benefit. Question if they are warranted.

In the space of presence found in each moment, free will is available, where we direct thought of heart and mind for good. We choose how we want our life to feel and create our world through visualisation. Whatever your constant subconscious focus is, positive or negative, you will receive if you hold the feelings steady for long enough.

Imagine you are looking for a new job. On paper, you are perfectly qualified for the role.

"They will never give me the job at the company. There will be so many applicants, all eminently more qualified than I am. If only I had more experience, I might have a chance."

or:

"I look forward to being the successful new hire at the company. I feel so excited and honoured to be part of such a dynamic team. I am eager to start and make a positive contribution."

Which statement carries the most power?

The answer is, they both do. Can you imagine how these scenarios are likely to play out? We create our future by the thoughts we allow to dominate our feelings. There isn't a rule saying only positive thinking will become manifest!

That which we consciously create from feeling and visualisation makes our future. We often run on auto-pilot without conscious creation, hoping to end up at the 'right' destination. As you direct your future, at this moment, you have foreknowledge of what will be. You cannot know all variations because others are creating their reality around you. Be in presence, accepting of what is.

When will 'Now' become the moment you take your first step into the life you want to live? The same old patterns of thinking will likely result in the same old ways of life. Your feeling, created by the labels you place on yourself compared to others, creates your expectation for failure or success. You can be wonderfully extraordinary, exceeding your expectations if that is your wish.

Allow thoughts different from your norm, even if they seem difficult or near impossible. You do not need to know the whole picture about your desired destination, only how you want to feel and the first step you will take. Have confidence that where there is a will, there is a way. Embrace the exciting changes–you can do it. Catch negative gremlins of 'I can't because' and 'others can do it better' etc. and challenge them, crushing them one by one. Does that need to stop you from moving forward? Maybe others could do something better, but you do it best in your way.

**Trust that you have all the wisdom
to know what you must do and when.
Ask, be still, and listen in the silence.**

Step into your power:

- Both the conscious and subconscious direction of our energy creates our future.
- Train your subconscious to focus on positive thought patterns.
- Visualise and feel what you want to experience.
- FEELING and VISUALISATION direct our future.

Heart, mind and soul in unison

When heart, mind and soul are in unison,
miracles happen.
Live in the emotion of how you will feel
when your dream is a reality.

Let go of the details of how it will
come into existence,
knowing that your dream is already in production.

Be attached to this feeling.
Be in the flow, trusting your intuition.
Be flexible to changes and diversions along the way.

You are more powerful than you know.
YOU ARE THE CREATOR WITHIN.

Rediscover The Creator Within

nineteen

Step into your power

Creating your world takes practice. From not noticing your thoughts, you move to consciously creating the world you see around you, filling it with gifts of your choice. With focus, yet with little effort, your empowering thoughts become your chosen feelings. Feeling & visualisation are your superpowers.

Your brain believes what you tell it and only understands the present tense. Visualise your future as if the things you want are already yours. What empowering thoughts can you 'add' to yourself to drive you forward positively?

- What do you want? If you are unsure, how do you want to feel?
- What are your life goals?
- Where would you like to be in 10 years?

- What would you do if you only had six months to live?
- What if you only have today?

Take time to focus on each question in turn. Direct your imagination and hone an image of your desired life. What do you want to be part of your world? What affirmations are empowering?

Write down your wishes to add clarity to your thinking and allow your imagination and intuition to engage. Commitment to these visions during meditation can further help integrate these positive ideas into your psyche.

When we make changes, our ego will block our path to keep us within familiar behaviour patterns. As a result, it may tell us that it is not possible to make significant changes. Are you going to listen this time?

As you create your vision for what you want in life, challenge yourself to notice if you are making up stories of possible calamities to prevent your first step. Are there blocks you have carried with you, believing them wholeheartedly to be accurate? Will you choose, in awareness, to make changes?

For example, the subject of money is a block for many:

- Money is the source of all evil.
- Money doesn't grow on trees.
- Money corrupts.
- Rich people are greedy.
- Money invites jealousy.
- It is better to be poor and happy than rich and sad.
- Money can't buy happiness.
- Our family has always struggled with money.
- Spiritual people are not interested in money.

Do these sayings lead to a positive mindset regarding finances? Can you see how such thoughts can block your path to financial abundance? What we resist persists.

If any of the following lists of ideas do not resonate and trigger negative thoughts, challenge yourself to question why that may be—bearing in mind that not all will apply to your circumstances and stages of life. For example, are you making a comparison to others to feel more or less than you believe yourself to be?

Choose your affirmations wisely and add your own, drawn from your heart, mind and soul:

- "Money flows easily and freely to me through good fortune for the good of all."
- "I make time for my dreams, and the bills take care of themselves."
- "I am equal to all others."
- "I am enough."
- "I am deserving of love and happiness."
- "I do not need to know the big picture, only my first step. I trust I have all the wisdom I need. I wait in stillness, ask for guidance and listen."
- "I take my first step. My feelings carry me with flow and passion in my experience."
- "I know where I am going, and I trust I will reach my goal. The steps become clear at the right time."
- "Now is my time to step into my power & take action."
- "All I give of myself is returned and more besides. I give compassion, knowing I grow in compassion, love knowing I grow in love...".
- "When I am excited and focused, I am good at everything I set my mind to."
- "Learning comes to me intuitively."

- "My physical pain subsides as I focus on my passions."
- "I live in presence, in bliss, love and joy."

Manifest the life you wish to live in:

- You are now moving from not noticing thought to consciously creating the world you see around you.
- You do not need to know what you want in life, only how you wish to feel.
- With focus, thoughts become your chosen feelings.
- When we make changes in our minds, our egos will put blocks in our path to keep us within past behaviour patterns.
- Positive affirmations are empowering.
- The brain only understands the present tense. Visualise your future as if the things you want are already yours.
- If you stumble in your plans, what is stopping you? Your thoughts of the past or future, or the negative labels you have given yourself?
- You can conceive anything you perceive.

Rediscover The Creator Within

twenty

Make your dreams come true

Visualisation and feelings are your superpowers

B y now, you are uncovering the lies you tell yourself that keep you small and struggling against the flow of life. Is it your time to stop sleepwalking through life? It takes conscious effort to create your future. Who do you want to become? Ask, "Who would I become if resources and skills had no limit?"

The only limit is your imagination.

The suggestion that 'visualisation and feelings are your superpowers' can be considered by many as nonsense. In some ways, they are correct. There is no sensory perception, (non-sense) touch, feel, taste, sight or sound involved in creating our future in free will. We use imagination and intuitive feeling.

For example, if you place your hand on a loved one's shoulder, this touch may fill you with love and positive emotion. However, if you touch the shoulder of a stranger, you are unlikely to feel the same. So what is creating your experience, your senses, or your imagination and feeling about the experience?

Thought, feeling and visualisation create your world. It goes beyond all we have discovered thus far. If not instantaneously, you can manifest objects at will (think Leonardo Da Vinci rather than David Copperfield). Although this may sound bonkers, an individual like you or I conceived all human-made things in imagination, so stay with me. For example, the Mona Lisa, submarines, aeroplanes, and infrared vision were made possible within the laws of physics and were born from a dream. All artificial objects are projections of thought made physical. Your home and prized possessions are yours because you first dreamed of them and honed your thinking and imagination for their acquisition. We create our relationships, skill sets, livelihood and hobbies from a desire to experience a particular feeling that, at the outset, only exists in our imagination. Visualising the future brings all possibilities into your awareness, opening your mind to opportunities.

The space that negative thoughts and feelings leave allows the 'right' decisions to be made, with heart and mind working together. So often, the heart knows what it wants before the mind falls in line and adds to life's flow.

Thoughts from the head become feelings.
Ideas from the heart are born in feeling.

The noise of our self-limiting beliefs too often drowns out the heart. Sit still with your hand on your heart and ask, what do I want to feel? What do I want to experience? Take time to imagine your life in this feeling.

Long-held negative beliefs will surface, but you have the choice to listen or turn them around to your advantage. When we create the future we want, it doesn't feel like hard work and life flows without effort.

Imagination builds a picture of what you want to create in your world through feeling. Heart, mind, and soul working together bring all you dream of to your physical reality. As a result of this symbiosis, you are as expansive as you wish to be.

Every journey starts with a first step. You do not need to know where you are going, but you need to know how you want to feel. Quieten thought, and life flows. You have all the wisdom you need inside you. There is so much to be discovered and indeed rediscovered about the condition of being human.

Dream a dream:

- It takes a CONSCIOUS effort to create the future of our choice. We access consciousness here, in this moment, by grounding ourselves in presence.
- We are not our thoughts, yet feelings and visualisation create our experience and become our personal world.
- Feeling and visualisation are our superpowers.
- Life unfolds–we alone are responsible for choosing how we experience it.
- Visualising the future brings all possibilities into our awareness, opening our minds to new opportunities.
- When heart, mind and soul work in unison, all things are possible in the flow of life.
- We can't change the world, but we can change our world.
- You are the creator within.

Rediscover The Creator Within

Mindfulness and Meditation

twenty one

Practice to presence

A clear mind allows good focus
and well-directed decisions.

There are layers to presence, and the more we practice, the better we are at the game of life. How would you fare in a city centre lost in thoughts of your to-do list whilst driving? How would a professional sportsperson perform if their mind wandered? Must their heads be in the game? This ability to focus entirely on what we are doing is the surface level of presence, easily attainable when in the moment, in the flow of life.

We experience our whole existence inside us. Everything outside us is a fabrication of our minds, our senses being the transducers from the perceived physical world, taking information via a receptive field for the brain to translate. Everything we see, touch, taste, smell, see or hear, we experience within us as our brains interpret this sensory information. This book will go some way to explaining how our thoughts shape our personal worlds, running within the subconscious in a predetermined pattern until we become enlightened to our free will.

When we are in a safe environment, the senses can be calm, and nothing is required of us that the body doesn't already interpret. Hence our senses are a gateway to slowing thought and moving to stillness and presence. Breath also happens without the need for conscious thought. By 'watching' our breathing, our mind can be distracted from the programs of the subconscious.

Some suddenly find themselves in presence when all the mind noise stops—most work to find their way. The more you practice stillness, the easier it becomes.

When you attempt to silence thought, you can expect to become acutely aware of the constant mind chatter. When you start noticing your thoughts, pat yourself on the back, you have made the first step into presence.

The moment we notice ourselves caught in
thoughts of the past or future,
we have leapt towards presence.

When you find yourself attending and becoming embroiled in your thoughts, breathe deeply into your body and become the observer. As you breathe out, breathe away your thoughts. Feel the relaxation and peace that falls into you.

Meditation comes in many guises, and there is always time to practice. Studying a flower's perfection for as little as 30 seconds is starting a journey to quieten the mind. The subconscious adds commentary such as 'this is a yellow flower, a buttercup,' etc. Notice these thoughts and let them float away by moving into feeling about what you are experiencing at that moment.

Mindfulness is a way to begin creating space for empowering thought that will serve you, directed by you, from a place of peace and love.

Rediscover The Creator Within

twenty two

I come to my senses

From thought to feeling

Practices to settle the mind:

1. For as little as 30 seconds, look at a flower, a blade of grass, a log, or a rock.

2. Walk through nature, letting it fill your senses. Be aware of sounds, smells, physical feelings, beauty and taste, focusing on one sense at a time.

3. Pick something in nature and question its place. What purpose does it serve?

4. Sit in the sunshine and feel the warm rays. Close your eyes if you feel comfortable doing so.

5. Sit, walk or lie in the fresh air and take deep breaths.

6. Eyes open or closed, become aware of each breath as it enters and exits your body; take deep breaths from your core to the top of your head.

   • Breathe in until your body chooses to breathe out.

   • Breathe out until your body decides to breathe in.

7. As you sit with your eyes closed (open if you are not comfortable) for several minutes, bring your awareness to something from each of the senses in turn. Notice the sensation of your bottom and legs on the chair—the feeling of your clothing. What can you hear? What can you smell? Can you taste anything in the air?

8. Think of someone or something or somewhere that fills you with love in an uncomplicated way. Notice your feelings.

9. Stare at 1 o'clock over a tree or bush with a clear background (not bright sun). Notice any thoughts that arise in this space, then re-focus on the tree.

10. Gaze at the flames of a fire or a candle.

11. Sit with eyes closed and count back from 5:

     •   5—relax all the muscles in your face around your eyes and mouth.

     •   4—relax your jaw, letting your tongue rest lightly behind your upper teeth.

     •   3—relax your shoulders and arms.

     •   2—relax your back and abdomen.

     •   1—relax your legs.

12. Close your eyes and stand with your feet comfortably apart, eyes closed.

     •   Gently lean forward and then back several times.

     •   Come back to a still point.

     •   Gently sway left then right a few times.

     •   Come back to your point of stillness.

     •   Open your eyes when you are ready.

13. Close your eyes, take deep breaths, put your hand on your heart. Sit in patient stillness. If thoughts arise, use the out-breath to imagine blowing them gently away.

14. Announce within or without "I have this thank you" or "I trust and respect myself in awareness of this moment".

15. Listen to a guided meditation (but not when driving or operating machinery).

16. Practice yoga.

17. Practice the gratitude exercise.

18. Practice Tai Chi.

19. Practice deep listening. Listen to someone, intently giving your full attention from a deep and reflective space within you. If thoughts arise on responding, let them go and allow the other person to continue their dialogue. Make a great effort to hear what is beyond their words by not adding your commentary. Your aim is for support and understanding, not necessarily agreement.

20. Use online Mindfulness Apps.

I come to my senses

twenty three

Meditation

Coming to your senses away from thoughts
of the past and future takes practice.
Be patient with yourself.

Meditation is sitting in stillness with no involvement in thought and without focusing on a particular question you wish to have answered. It is very powerful when practised regularly. Ideas may come and go, but once you have completed reading this book, you will be able to recognise them as just that; thought and not your reality. When thoughts become quiet, you have the infinite space to create the future you wish to live.

If you want a burden lifted, a question answered, or a problem solved, ask in prayer or meditation. Wait in the silence and watch patiently for answers. Sometimes you will receive a message in meditation. Other times be vigilant, and your response will become apparent in the

225

days ahead. This idea may sound implausible, but meditation is a way of accessing your depths without all the needless mind chatter. You can find inspiration and flow in meditation—all the answers you ever need are available to you.

Binaural beats music, sounds of nature, sound bowls or chanting in meditation are excellent aids to quieten the mind. These are pointers, and you will find your way with experience. In time, you may lie down, but beginners will often find they drift off into sleep.

Introduction to meditation:

- Sit comfortably on a chair or cross-legged with your spine long and straight.
- Head straight ahead with the ears over your shoulders. A head tilted backwards will lead you into thinking, and your head forwards may cause you to fall asleep.
- Nose in line with the navel.
- Engage stomach muscles and sit tall and strong. Use a pillow under your buttocks and/or as a lumbar support if necessary for comfort.
- Eyes can be open with a soft gaze a couple of meters away or closed, turning softly inwards and upwards to the space between your eyebrows.
- Ensure you are sitting tall, straight, strong and comfortable.

Meditate for as long as you wish. There is no right or wrong, only what suits you.

Here follows an example of a way into meditation:

- Start by noticing your thoughts. They are always there as we enter meditation, and some days will be busier than others. Slow your breath and close your eyes if you are comfortable doing so. Take three deep, slow, long breaths.
- Move into relaxation by imagining ten steps in front of you.
- With each deep breath, 'step down' and become more relaxed from top to toe:

1. *Scalp:* With your first imaginary step-down, breathe into the top of your head. As you breathe out, relax your scalp.

2. *Forehead & fine lines:* Breathe into the top of your head. Breathe out, and relax your forehead and the fine lines around the eyes.

3. *Jaw:* Breathe into the top of your head. Breathe out, and relax your jaw, resting your tongue behind your top teeth.

4. *Neck and shoulders:* Breathe into the top of your head. Breathe out and feel the release of tension in the neck and shoulders.

5. *Chest:* Breathe in, fully expanding the rib cage, then up to the top of your head. Release all tension in the chest as you breathe out.

6. *Abdomen:* Breathe in, expanding first the core, then the ribs. Release all tension from your stomach.

7. *Hips:* Repeating the full-body breath from the stomach's full expansion to the ribs and the head and releasing all tension in the hip area on exhalation.

8. *Legs:* Full body breath and on your exhalation release any tension in the legs, leaving them feeling completely relaxed.

9. *Toes:* Full body breath in and on exhalation, breathe down to your toes and notice energy tingling.

10. *Entire body, top of head to toes:* Breathe the full-body breath filling the abdomen, lungs to the top of your head. As you breathe out, feel a waterfall of relaxation falling from the top of your head to your toes as the whole body releases all tension.

These techniques help to distract the mind with non-thoughts:

- Imagine seven horizontal spinning rings in the colours of the rainbow.
  - Red, at your base, as you sit
  - Orange, at your navel
  - Yellow, at the solar plexus
  - Green, at your heart
  - Blue, at the throat
  - Indigo, in your head between your eyebrows
  - Violet, at the crown of your head
- Think of a bright white peaceful rod of energy passing through them from high above you and throughout your body as you sit tall and strong.
- Relax with each out-breath starting with the muscles in your face on your forehead and eyes. Work with your out-breaths, breathing out tension from every area of your body, in turn, jaw and neck, shoulders, arms, chest, abdomen, legs, down to your toes. As you breathe in, breathe in whatever you choose, e.g. I am love, wisdom, peace, etc.
- Imagine watching each of the colours spinning in turn, starting with red at your base and observe as the

colours become strong and fluid. Move up the rainbow colours until you can imagine a bright white light connecting you with all the knowledge and love of the Universe.

There is no right or wrong, and with practice, you will find the best method to help quieten your mind and come to presence.

Questions for enquiry/suggestions to meditate on:

1. What are the past and future?
2. What do I know about who 'I am' with 100% certainty?
3. If we have thoughts but are not our thoughts, who or what witnesses my thinking?
4. Who/what am I beyond thought?
5. "I create my world." What does that mean?
6. What is a trigger?
7. We can't change the world, but we can change our world.
8. What is wellbeing?
9. Is wellbeing innate?
10. Is love innate?
11. What is a judgement?
12. How can I add the most significant value to the world?

Ask & you will receive

When heart, mind & soul
are in unison & ask,
you will receive.

Printed in Great Britain
by Amazon